# Responding to Individual Needs:
# A Guide for Teachers

Volume I in the series

## Learning Potential

Edited by
Peter J. Gamlin

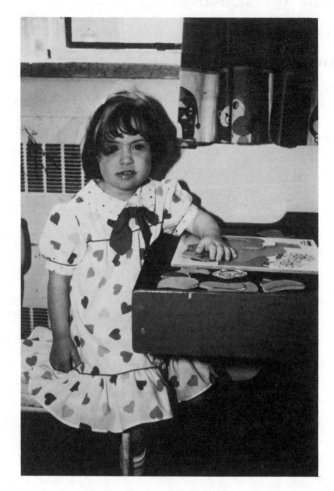

*Beth Ann*

# Responding to Individual Needs: A Guide for Teachers

*Peter J. Gamlin*
Department of Applied Psychology
Ontario Institute for Studies in Education
University of Toronto

*D. Russell Fleming*
Faculty of Education
University of Toronto

C. J. Hogrefe, Inc.

Lewiston, NY · Toronto

**Library of Congress Cataloging in Publication Data**

Gamlin, Peter J., 1941–
Responding to individual needs.

Learning potential ; v. 1)
Bibliography: p.
Includes indexes.

1. Education, Primary.  2. Readiness for school.  3. Individualized instruction.  4. Group work in education.  I. Fleming, D. Russell, 1935–  II. Title.  III. Series.

LB1511.G36   1985                372.12'5                85-8414
ISBN 0-88937-010-9

**Canadian Cataloguing in Publication Data**

Gamlin, Peter J., 1941–
Responding to individual needs

(Learning potential ; 1)
Bibliography: p.
Includes indexes.
ISBN 0-88937-010-9

1. Educational psychology.  2. Cognition in children.  3. Learning ability.  I. Fleming, David Russell, 1935–
II. Title.  III. Series.

LB1051.G35   1985                370.15'23                C85-098671-0

To
Dianna
and
Lauraine

# Preface

A teacher's main concern is to respond to the individual needs of his or her students. Many teachers feel that they can more successfully achieve this goal when there are fewer than fifteen students in the classroom. However, this does not guarantee that a better job of teaching will be accomplished, or conversely, that students will become more effective learners. What teachers need to understand are the skills that each student brings to learning tasks. This understanding will take into account both the cognitive skills and the emotional development of the student. This book will explore the development of these skills for children three years of age through adolescence with particular emphasis on the years three to eight.

Working one to one or in very small groups of two or three students makes it more likely that attention is given to the student's learning process as well as to the student's emotional needs. However, when working with class sizes of 15 to 30 or more students, it becomes increasingly difficult to do this. Despite large class sizes, most teachers do attempt to respond to individual needs. They do this in many ways, for example, by teaching around problems that the majority of students are experiencing, by having students working with other students in small groups or by using instructional material that can be tailored to individual needs.

This book will help teachers respond to individual needs by giving them a means for grouping children who are similar with respect to their learning process. Specifically, this book will focus on "similarity thinking" as a way to document where students are in their learning process. The possible groupings suggested are therefore not only based on children's ability to pass "tests" of achievement, but also based on the potential of students to think through learning tasks in certain ways.

This is an interactive approach to grouping students in that students at a particular place in the development of similarity thinking will have certain kinds of problems with certain kinds of learning tasks. We think that this is a better approach to grouping students because it not only takes into account what students can do by way of achievement, it also takes into account the thinking or learning process they employ as they respond to learning tasks.

Another distinctive feature of this book is the emphasis we give to the emotional development of the child. The emotional development of the child is described in the chapter "Therapy for the 'Sane' Child", which in part, outlines the security theory of William Blatz. We focus on the degree to which a child is independently or dependently secure. Again, the reader will notice that we take an interactive approach. For example, children who are independently secure take risks with learning such that they benefit from the consequences of their actions. They interpret corrective feedback positively, as constructive criticism, and in this way demonstrate that they are learning how to learn. Dependently secure children, on the other hand, typically interpret corrective feedback as a negative commentary on their ability to learn because they need approval from others. Consequently they do not take the risks associated with learning how to learn. Although dependently secure children may have the potential to learn with respect to similarity thinking, they will not realize that potential until they become independently secure.

In summary, this book gives experienced and prospective teachers a framework for assessing children's potential to learn, taking into account cognitive skills, specifically similarity thinking skills, as well as the emotional status of children, particularly the development of independent security. The teacher who wants to take into account the individual needs of children, including both cognitive skills and emotional development will be able to do a better job of grouping these children so as to provide them with instruction that is matched to their learning skills.

The book introduces the reader to complex ideas by using anecdotes and practical examples showing how similarity thinking can be used in the classroom. We place a special emphasis on the development of planning skills showing how children must organize their thinking in order to plan ahead. We also identify questioning techniques that stimulate thinking and planning. The final chapters of the book bring all of the concepts together in a case study which is followed by recommendations to the classroom teacher and the educational consultant. Consequently, teachers and consultants will discover new ways to talk to parents.

Russ Fleming has been a classroom teacher for 24 years including many years with the Institute of Child Study, University of Toronto. Presently, he is a professor at the Faculty of Education, University of Toronto, where he instructs student teachers. Dr. Fleming uses his expertise as a former classroom teacher to show how similarity thinking applies to classroom activities. Peter Gamlin began his association with Dr. Fleming at the Institute of Child Study as a professor of child psychology. Dr. Gamlin has been a professor at the Ontario Institute for Studies in Education, University of Toronto, for 15 years where he has been developing the model of similarity thinking as well as applying his model in research, teaching, private practice and with various boards of education.

# Acknowledgments

This book could not have come about without assistance from many individuals. We would like to thank Roslyn and Victor Vincent and their children Brian and Beth Ann. We are especially grateful for having had the opportunity to work with Beth Ann who is simply a delight to be with. We thank the staff of the Metropolitan Toronto Association for the Mentally Retarded as well as the teachers of Woodgreen Neighbourhood House nursery school. We would also like to thank the principal and staff of Pauline Public School who allowed us to conduct preliminary work on the assessment of similarity thinking. Thanks also go to Nick Laidlaw who encouraged us to link the "security theory" of William Blatz to similarity thinking. We want also to acknowledge the help of Maria Cantalini and Rosa Sentino who participated in the interview reported in Chapter 8. Maria also designed the background design task described in Chapter 6. Dianna Fleming has made a significant contribution to this work by sharing her expertise, experience and wonderful examples of kindergarteners playing and learning. Lauraine Robertson has laboured long and hard making a significant difference to our efforts by providing the case study of Richard and allowing us to use a summary of her doctoral research reported in Chapter 5. She has also given unstintingly of her time and energy helping to edit the manuscript. The typing of the manuscript was no easy task since deadlines always approach more quickly than one expects. We thank Silvanira Rizwan for working diligently to make certain that this goal was achieved.

Peter J. Gamlin
D. Russell Fleming

# Contents

# Chapter 1

# Introducing Beth Ann

In Chapter 1 we introduce a case study of a child with a severe learning problem to make the point that every child shares with all children similar kinds of learning processes. Our definition of learning potential extends to all children: those with learning disabilities and those with normal or even gifted abilities. Beth Ann's situation underlines how important it is to understand both the learning process and the emotionality of the child because this kind of understanding makes it possible to program for individual needs.

Recently we enjoyed a June evening with Victor and Roslyn Vincent. We were sitting on the back step talking about their children, Brian and Beth Ann. As the conversation developed it became obvious that they put the highest priority into raising their children. For example Victor described a week's activities for Brian, their seven year old son which included tap-dancing lessons, followed by soccer, an evening with the Beavers, and ended with music lessons.

The conversation turned to Beth Ann, the four year old member of the family who Roslyn described as her "Mighty-mite". As she began to talk about Beth Ann her motherly love and pride in her daughter's accomplishments became obvious. She described how Beth Ann had recently learned to pile up boxes in the kitchen to get to the cookie jar which was on the counter much above her reach. She described how alarmed she was to discover that Beth Ann could reach over the fence to unlock the gate. Beth Ann is very fleet of foot and before Roslyn knew what was happening, her daughter had disappeared through the gate and down the laneway toward the main road. Fortunately, she had seen her child's head bobbing along over the top of the fence and dashed out of the door in time to retrieve her from the driveway.

It was obvious to us that the Vincents are a healthy and productive family, developing interests together and enjoying life. From the way their family is thriving it is not apparent that one family member, Beth Ann, is a child with Down's Syndrome. Only a few· short years ago children with Down's Syndrome were considered so severely mentally retarded that there was no hope for a normal life. Present methods of early intervention that include recent advances in educational methods and medical knowledge have changed the life chances of such children so that a normal style is more attainable. The new programs designed to develop the learning potential of mentally retarded children have improved dramatically. At four years of age Beth Ann has already spent two years in the Woodgreen Neighbourhood House nursery school. This nursery school is run by the Metropolitan Toronto Association for the Mentally Retarded and is a special program which is meant to give mentally retarded children early stimulation. This book introduces an approach that will add significantly to the effectiveness of these kinds of programs. In particular we give new meaning to our understanding of learning or human potential.

## How Will Beth Ann Fare in Life?

Victor and Roslyn openly discussed their expectations for Beth Ann. They said that they expected no less for her than for their son Brian. Their greatest hope for both children is that they will grow up to have high self esteem. Independence is an important goal. They hoped that Brian and Beth Ann would learn to care for themselves and be productive members of society.

When we asked Victor and Roslyn what they had learned about raising children, given that they have a child with Down's Syndrome, they both laughed and Victor said, "Everything! Everything that we took for granted before."

Roslyn told us how she had learned the importance of many little things, like stimulating Beth Ann's eye movements, and working with her daily as an infant to get her to produce the head movements that had come so naturally to Brian. Beth Ann required special exercises and routines to get her to sit up, and even the vocalization of sounds that other children make as a matter of course, became significant. Initially Beth Ann was unable to learn anything on her own. Everything demanded a routine, a method. Most importantly, Roslyn had to know what step came next in order to help Beth Ann. Now, with the support of a stimulating environment Beth Ann is learning new things every day.

Despite the extra care that Beth Ann required, her parents learned that "all kids are different". For example, Beth Ann took less time for toilet training than Brian. This observation was surprising but revealing to her parents. They said that before Beth Ann was born thay had no idea about the variation in the development of children.

Now Victor and Roslyn try to persuade other parents at Home and School meetings and elsewhere not to expect their children to develop at the same rate. They try to point out the dangers of making excessive demands without taking the child's development into consideration. The positive experiences Victor and Roslyn have had with Beth Ann has helped them reach out to other parents.

## Now That Beth Ann is 4 Years Old

Now that Beth Ann is four, it is time to think of the next step in her life. Her parents are already thinking ahead to the time when she will be five and going to kindergarten with the other children in the neighbourhood. The Vincent's are very careful parents. They do not want to send her to kindergarten until she has been thoroughly prepared for the experience. They feel that insufficient preparation would neither be fair to Beth Ann nor to the kindergarten teacher.

In consultation with the people at the Toronto Association for the Mentally Retarded, Beth Ann's parents have decided to take a number of steps to prepare her for the kindergarten experience. She is attending an integrated playroom class two afternoons per week following nursery school. This activity is very important for her social development since she has not learned to play cooperatively with other children. Many four years old still play along-side, rather than with, another child. The remaining three afternoons in the school week Beth Ann spends at home with her mother. Unlike children from regular nursery programs Beth Ann's program extends into the home. At Beth Ann's nursery school, teachers make regular home visits. During these visits, the teacher reviews the child's school progress with the parents. The parents and teacher together agree on home activities which will reinforce this progress. For instance, if behaviour is a problem and the school is trying a new routine to make a change, the parents become aware of the teaching procedures and reinforce them at home. As a final preparation for kindergarten, Beth Ann will go to an integrated day care center so that she can be introduced to the activities of other children her own age.

## What Can Beth Ann Understand?

If you ask Beth Ann how old she is, like most young children who have just had their fourth birthday, she will say that she is three. With a bit of coaching her parents are confident she will soon be able to tell you that she is four. She also knows that she is a "girl" if you ask her whether she is a girl or a boy. Like most children with Down's Syndrome the development of tongue and vocal muscles prevents her from articulating many words clearly, so you have to listen quite carefully if you are to understand what she is saying.

Beth Ann is beginning to know her own body quite well. When Joanne, her nursey school teacher, names a body part such as her foot or hand, Beth Ann can point to it quite readily. Her teacher is proud of the fact that Beth Ann has learned to point to six major parts of her body. She can name these parts but only when the teacher points to them.

Her drawing skill is also improving. When she draws a person, like many children her age, she draws only a head with several unorganized features, such as eyes, nose and mouth. When Roslyn sits down with her and talks about where each part should go, she can draw quite a good face, but she does need some help.

Although in our view similarity thinking is one of the most important learning skills any child can acquire, many other kinds of understanding make it possible for children to make the best use of this kind of thinking. As children develop they acquire many concepts, e.g. colour, size and amount. They also begin to learn how to plan and use language. Beth Ann has made several important advances in these areas which we discuss below.

## Colour

Like many pre-kindergarten children Beth Ann cannot name five colours, but when her mother holds up coloured blocks and asks her what colour they are she can provide the names red, blue, and yellow. She has developed quite good matching skills for all colours and can sort identical colours into groups. The fact that Beth Ann can sort and match but cannot name all the colours reveals much about the depth of her understanding since these tasks are not of equal difficulty. For instance it is much easier to match colours and to sort objects by colour than it is to identify a colour by a sound such as a word. The fact that she has already learned the names of some of the colours shows that she is progressing. At this point, teaching Beth Ann new colour words would be an appropriate activity. Naturally, the more colours that are introduced, the more difficult the task becomes. It can be expected that learning the words appropriate for additional colours will take longer and require more practice.

Learning new colours is easier when they are introduced in matching tasks. Two blocks of different colours are placed in front of the child. The adult says the name of one of the colours. The child learns to match the name to the colour. Once a number of colours are learned in this manner the child can be given several additional coloured blocks to choose from at one time. The child must listen to the colour name and point to the correct colour block. The child should also say the name of a colour after the adult says it or say the name of a colour when it is selected from an array of different coloured blocks.

Once the child is naming and discriminating the colours, the adult can use a single block at a time and hold it in front of the child. Colours that are recognized should be used first and only after some practice should the new coloured blocks be introduced. Hints, such as the sound of the first letter are important clues for helping the child retrieve a name. More hints should be used at the beginning of the learning sessions and reduced progressively. For example, the whole name is used in the beginning followed by part of the colour name which in turn is followed by using only the initial consonant sound. Finally, after much practice the child is encouraged to produce the word spontaneously when the coloured block is shown.

## *Size*

Like most children, Beth Ann's performance is not always the same at home and at school. At home, Roslyn has found that Beth Ann can go to the table when told and select the bigger glass and return with it. At school, Joanne says Beth Ann is only able to sort things into groups of "big" and "little". She does this as a matching task in which she has both a large object and a small one in front of her and she places other objects in either the large object group or the small object group.

There are many subtle differences that exist between the home and the school that do not transfer from one place to the other. Teachers should not be surprised to find that parents talk about performance at home that is different from performance at school. Sometimes it is impossible or undesirable to tranfer a particular skill from the home to the school or vice versa. For instance, although Beth Ann has the ability to dress herself at home in familiar surroundings, she has problems completing this task at school where there is the distraction of other children. Both teachers and parents should know that such differences do exist and be prepared to talk about them.

## *Planning*

Getting dressed requires quite a bit of planning. The child has to start somewhere, which early on usually depends upon where the adult thinks the starting point should be. The child must then select clothes according to which one fits over or next to another.

At home Beth Ann can put on her underwear and socks as well as pull up her pants but sometimes she gets her arm into her sweater the wrong way. At this point she needs help. She is not able to put on her shoes yet.

At the nursery school, where expectations are somewhat different because of the number of children who must be dressed at one time, she often does not attend to the task long enough to complete dressing. She has to be helped to finish pulling up her pants and she also has problems with her sweater. Beth Ann will eventually learn to perform these tasks with other children around her.

Beth Ann's ability to dress herself indicates that she is acquiring a relative sense of planning. That is, she is beginning to come to terms with how things are organized around her. At present she understands them from a functional point of view; what she does, she knows about. First she understands how her own body parts are organized in relationship to each other and then she transfers that knowledge to other things such as when she draws people with body parts.

We observed her working with two different puzzles. Her approach convinced us that she is acquiring the ability to transfer knowledge. For instance, in one puzzle the picture of a man was divided into three separate rectangular pieces. The puzzle was assembled by placing the pieces in the correct order, one under the other. The top piece was composed of the shoulders and head, the middle piece the man's trunk, and the lower piece the legs. She assembled the three pieces by starting with the head and working down the body. The head is the part of the body that she knows best (as can be understood from watching her draw). She knows the other parts of the body less well, but understands their relative position.

Another puzzle of a man was divided vertically and horizontally into four pieces. She could not solve this puzzle since she had to understand that pieces not only went over and under each other but also beside other pieces.

We also saw her assemble a jig-saw puzzle. The pieces of the puzzle formed the picture of a farmer and they were put together by placing them into a framework for organizing the pieces. The framework provides extra hints for arranging the pieces. Again she started with the

6

head and worked out from there to include other parts of the body that she was familiar with. She found the puzzle difficult because she had to place the pieces vertically as well as horizontally. In spite of the framework she found it too difficult to organize the pieces. As a result she found it necessary to resort to trial and error.

Beth Ann is beginning to transfer her intuitive sense of planning to language. With her mother's help she can place a block "in front", "behind", or "beside" another block. In the nursery school Joanne can tell her to place a block "in", "on" or "under" another block and she performs very well.

Getting dressed, solving puzzles and understanding prepositions are important examples of planning skills. In Beth Ann's case these skills are still very rudimentary. However, they are indicative of a potential which needs to be developed.

### Amount

Beth Ann understands the concept of "some" when used in the context of a familiar task, like "Bring me some cherries". In response to this request she usually brings a handful of cherries. However she would probably not differentiate between the concept of "some" and "many". She would probably give you the same number of cherries if you asked her for "many" cherries as she would when you asked for "some" cherries.

The ability to designate objects by pointing is an important one. In very young children it often precedes the use of speech to signify objects. As yet, Beth Ann cannot point to individual blocks placed in a row as she counts them. Her rote counting of numbers has developed for the first five consecutive numbers. Given this level of understanding it is clear that Beth Ann is some way from understanding the "cardinal principle" of number, e. g., that the last block counted is the total amount including everything that came before. In a social situation Beth Ann has no trouble understanding what it means to be the first in line for cookies. However, she experiences more difficulty performing tasks with less functional social meaning, such as pointing to the "first" and "last" blocks in a row.

### Language

Learning in school settings from junior kindergarten on is facilitated when language is used to mediate childrens' activities. Although children can be taught to match quite complex items without using language it is extremely important to introduce words into this learning process. Language use in a task (such as a matching) results in the child's understanding that one concept can be related to other concepts. For instance, Beth Ann's use of the word "middle" is at present a name word which serves only to point to a place on her body, which is named "your middle". It is not a relational term that allows her to find the middle of something else not even in the puzzle which showed the middle of a man. However, as the teacher intervenes to teach her how to use "middle" in solving puzzles and in other tasks she will gradually learn the generalized meaning of the word.

## Similarity Thinking

In our view the ability to make similarity judgements is one of the most important developments in the intellectual life of children. This ability begins in one form when children are very young and continually develops throughout their lifetime. Similarity thinking initially involves seeing how things go together even when they do not look exactly the same. Objects are put into collections where everything can be related to everything else, for example, things may be related on the basis of a similar colour or shape. Later on, with the ability to classify, children add to their understanding that things can be put into similar groups even when they look quite different. For example, grapes and peaches can be put together because they are both examples of the class fruit. Still later, children understand that quite different things can be compared for their similarity by using analogy and metaphor. For example, they will understand the sentence, "The river is a snake" when quite literally rivers cannot be snakes. We make no presumptions about how far Beth Ann can move in this kind of development. We emphasize similarity thinking because it is fundamental to being able to generalize what is learned in one situation so as to apply it in another; for example, what is learned at home and applied at school. In order to generalize or *transfer* old learning to new situations, the child must understand how the situations are similar. The child must understand when old learning can be used. Yellow things can be put together because they are yellow; grapes can be put with peaches because they are fruit; rivers can be put with snakes because they are both long and twisty. The child builds bridges between things and ideas on the basis of similarity judgements.

We decided to try Beth Ann's similarity thinking skills on a matching task. Usually we have junior kindergarten children match pictures, but Beth Ann is not developmentally ready for this task so we

8

decided to use three-dimensional toy materials. The use of toys in our approach coincided with her training at the nursery school. Two "target" objects were placed slightly apart on a table in front of her. She was handed objects one at a time and asked to place them with one or other of the targets on the basis of whether the object either "went with" or matched the target.

Beth Ann's matching ability is at very literal level. For example she cannot yet understand a task which asks her to select a toy from among several (three) which is "most like" a target toy. While she has an understanding of both the words "more" and "like", she does not understand what they mean together, where "more like" means "more similar to". On the other hand, if you asked her if she would like "more" cookies, she would not hesitate in answering "yes", showing that she has an understanding of the word "more".

The development of "more like" and "most like" concepts is a critical milestone in Beth Ann's intellectual development. These concepts are the basis for the symbolic transfer of ideas. They are at the very center of understanding early primary school experiences. Children learn about "most like" concepts using concrete materials. With practice this understanding becomes a resource which can be used in new situations and more generally in problem solving. Many mentally retarded individuals have problems with similarity thinking and "most like" concepts. Consequently they understand things in piecemeal fashion and therefore cannot transfer their understanding to new situations. Each experience they encounter is put into a compartment. They cannot take what they have learned in one set of circumstances and use it productively to problem solve in another.

The use of language can be tremendously helpful as a child attempts to think about how one thing compares to another and how old learning can be used in new situations. The grade two child who calls a dragon fly a "patoon helicopter bug" is using well developed similarity thinking skills to transfer ideas learned while playing with toys and models to insects at the cottage. Language and experience with things cannot be separated. Knowledge of a word is acquired as one comes to understand the thing or event that it represents. The meaning of a word is like a group of nested boxed that fit one inside the other. Opening one box allows you to open others. Beth Ann has opened the meaning of the first box for the words "more" and "like", but the meaning of "more like" or "most like" will be found in other boxes that she has yet to open.

In the assessment we placed two toys in front of her on the table just out of arm's reach; one was a duck, the other a goose. One at a time we handed her the toys which were either the same or similar to the duck or goose on the table. The first duck that we handed her was exactly the same as the target duck and she quickly placed it with the target. Next, we handed her a goose which was identical to the target goose. She quickly placed it with the goose. The third object we handed her was a goose which was the same colour as the target goose but with small variations in the pattern. She placed this toy with the duck. Each of the other toys that we handed her she placed with the goose if it matched exactly, but if it did not match the goose, she placed it with the duck (whether it matched the duck exactly or not).

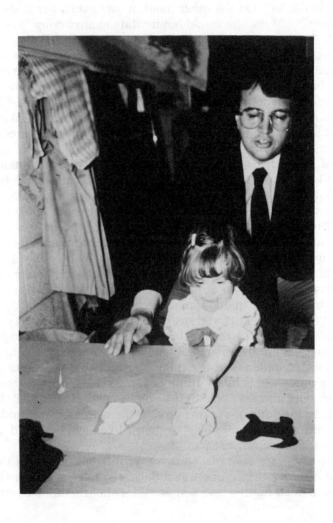

Beth Ann had decided to make two groups, one a group consisting of identical geese, the other of an assortment of toys, all of them different from each other. Two things are interesting in Beth Ann's response to this task. The first is her ability to discern small differences in quite complex patterns. The second is her decision to place quite different things together in another group. This system of grouping objects shows that she has developed a way of dealing with alternatives in planning her groupings. She is also beginning to notice similarities between things.

The ability to discern similarities and to plan ahead decisively are two important aspects of learning. At this point in her development Beth Ann has found a way of dealing with both of these learning strategies probably as a result of her training at the nursery school and the encouragement and practice she gets at home. So far the teaching of matching skills has been achieved non-verbally. This is an effective means of communicating ideas for two- and three-year olds. However, now that Beth Ann is getting ready for kindergarten, verbal mediation will be necessary to keep her abreast of the accelerated learning of the other kindergarten children.

Children use both equivalence matching and relative similarity thinking when they are able to identify pairs of objects. Verbal mediation will help the child learn how to pair objects. For example teachers can point out that in a pair of shoes a match is found in the mirror image of one shoe. Every detail of the target shoe must be mirrored in the second shoe in order to make a pair. Notice that one shoe is not exactly identical to the other since one fits on the right foot and the other fits on the left. They are similar however in that all the features in one are found in the other. The teacher can help the child understand the concepts of relative similarity and equivalence matching by using language that takes into account each individual child's ability to understand these concepts.

## Summary

This chapter describes Beth Ann's attempts to master a variety of activities such as assigning colour names, discriminating size differences, making judgements of amount and planning. This glimpse of Beth Ann's learning potential in various environments: home, nursery and playroom helps us understand the importance of the interaction between emotional and intellectual development. Beth Ann's parents and teachers believe in her potential to learn. They provide the external support system that makes it possible for her to exercise all of the learning skills described above, including similarity thinking. Similarity thinking makes it possible for Beth Ann to group things together even though they do not look exactly the same. This means that Beth Ann has a strategy for grouping things on the basis of "most like" even though at her present stage of development this understanding is intuitive. The continued practice of these skills will eventually enable Beth Ann to generalize from the old to the new. The "outside" support system of family and nursery school is facilitating the development of Beth Ann's "inside" feelings of security which in turn encourage her to practice these learning skills.

The concepts that we introduce in chapter one will be elaborated upon in later chapters. We explore these concepts by providing case studies of children at various stages in their cognitive emotional development.

Chapter one examined the learning potential of an exceptional child who is preparing for kindergarten. Chapter two provides teachers with a practical guide to determine every child's readiness for kindergarten. Teachers can use the information provided in the second chapter to respond in a more sensitive way to the individual needs of their students. In so doing they are better able to communicate with parents about the cognitive and emotional development of their children.

# Chapter 2

# Determining a Child's Readiness
# for Kindergarten

Chapter 1 showed how one little girl is preparing for kindergarten. This chapter is designed to help teachers talk to all parents about preparing their children for a positive school experience. While there are many different learning experiences that will prepare young children for school, we feel that one of the most important things children should learn is how to use their experiences from home to solve the new problems they will encounter in school. The ability to transfer experience from home to the school depends on the development of thinking, feeling and language skills which in turn directly affect the child's chances for success in school. We discuss the child's emotional development in more detail in chapters four and seven.

There are two parts to this chapter, the Performance Analysis and the Kindergarten Preparation:

i) The Performance Analysis describes the important cognitive skills which must be developed if a child is to be adequately prepared for kindergarten and afterwards in grades 1 and 2.

ii) The Kindergarten Preparation Questionnaire provides information for teachers about how the child behaves at home in various activities including the child at play and the child in everyday routines. The questionnaire results are most informative with respect to the child's social maturity. These are the social skills that teachers hope the child will be able to use in order to participate successfully in the kindergarten program.

## Performance Analysis

Traditionally, certain concepts have been identified as requiring development before a child is considered ready for kindergarten. These concepts include concept of self, the child's understanding of language (e.g., knowledge of the alphabet and certain grammatical structures) and various cognitive skill concepts such as size, number and colour. This more traditional approach to determining readiness

13

for kindergarten is piecemeal in that it does not provide a comprehensive treatment of the child's potential to learn. For example in many early identification programs the traditional approach does not take into consideration the child's experiences at home. Furthermore, these traditional approaches are not usually coordinated by theories that describe how a child develops and learns. In this chapter, we begin to show how information from the home can supplement information obtained from assessments done at school. We also begin to demonstrate how the model of Similarity Thinking provides the kind of theory that relates both cognitive skills and emotional development. In this chapter we outline the familiar notion of planning skills. However, it must be understood that similarity thinking is a prerequisite to the development of planning skills. As children develop and practice similarity thinking, they will become better planners.

The section on Performance Analysis initially introduces the teacher to the more traditional assessment concepts. We follow this introduction with a discussion of planning. The performance analysis is divided into five subsections: concepts of self, colour concepts, size concepts, number/amount concepts and the development of planning skills.

The age range for each item in the performance analysis does not indicate the earliest age at which children may be able to perform that particular activity. However, two things are suggested by including an age range: (1) that most children have progressed developmentally by that age and are able to perform the task, (2) that the particular activity is one which seems to be necessary for children's further learning.

## Concepts of Self

1. 3 yr. – Knowledge of a full name.
2. 3 yr. – Knowledge of own sex.
3. 3 yr. – Reference to the self as I.
4. 3 yr. – Knowledge of own age.
5. 3 yr. – Verbal expression of emotions, i.e., sad, happy, mad.
6. 3 yr. – Verbal knowledge of 6 to 10 body parts.
7. 3 yr. – Draw-a-man: Child can draw head and body or head with features.
8. 4 yr. – Child is able to assemble puzzle of a person demonstrating knowledge of body parts.
9. 5 yr. – Draw-a-man: Child draws a figure with head, body, arms, legs, feet, mouth, nose and eyes.
10. 5 yr. – Telling birthdate.

*Knowledge of full name:* By age three a child should be able to demonstrate an understanding of his or her own name by responding to the question, "What is your name?" When Beth Ann Vincent is asked this question she answers, "Beth V." She has not fully mastered this task, partly because the name Beth Ann has two components. However, she does answer to Beth Ann whenever someone is talking to her, indicating the ability to recognize at least the first part of her name. Beth Ann's parents will have to experiment and find out whether it is better to teach the full name or choose the shorter version before she goes to school. The important consideration here is that everyone, teachers, parents and other children, should be consistent (perhaps the use of the simpler name, Beth, will make the teaching task easier).

Beth Ann's knowledge of her full name helps to identify her and distinguish her from others. Once a child knows her name, she can understand that other people also have names. The ability to learn that other people have names as well, means that she is beginning to transfer knowledge – the key to all learning. Knowledge of names allows her to make an even more impressive step; the learning of pronouns. Once she has learned that she can be identified by a name, it will be easier to teach her pronouns such as "me", "I" and the possessive "mine".

*Knowledge of one's own sex:* Knowing one's own sex and being able to verbalize it is another important step in a child's development. Beth Ann knows that she is a girl because she can say "girl" when she is asked, "Are you a boy or a girl?" She also says that her brother is a "b" for boy (since she has trouble hearing the low tones in the rest of the word). Her ability to name her brother's sex is important because it shows that she is able to go beyond simply naming her brother. She is able to recognize another aspect of her brother, e.g., that he is a boy. Learning how to recognize someone of the opposite sex is an easier form of learning than pointing to someone who is similar, such as another girl. Vygotsky, a respected child psychologist, made this point as a result of his investigations:

> Our own experimental studies suggest that the child becomes aware of differences earlier than of likeness ... because awareness of similarity requires a more advanced structure of generalization and conceptualization than awareness of dissimilarity (1962, pp. 88-89).

What Beth Ann needs is practice in identifying which of her playmates are girls and which are boys. She should be encouraged to point at others when the word "boy" or "girl" is said and then be encouraged to say the words as she points. She must learn to physically point with her hand. Later she will learn to point in her speech.

*Reference to self as I:* Using I correctly in many different contexts indicates that the child has made important advances in thinking. When the child can use the pronoun "I", she is indicating that she wants to take some kind of initiative. Therefore we say that the use of the pronoun "I" usually indicates that the child is attempting to plan ahead. She wants to do something that has to be thought about ahead of time. Planning requires that the child:

1. Feels personally secure enough to act independently (see chapter seven).
2. Is capable of taking a personal initiative to make or do something.
3. Is capable of describing activities in advance of doing them.

Some young children, even those of kindergarten age, have difficulty referring to themselves as "I" when they are talking about initiating an activity. This is because the first person "I" is seldom modeled for young children by adults. Adults, most frequently, use "me" when they are actually involved in directing a child to do something, as when a parent says, "Give the soap to me." Since one of the ways children learn to use language is by modeling the language of the adults in their lives, they usually come to understand the use of the pronoun "me" first. It seems natural that children will use the words that they hear other people using.

A child can learn the use of the pronoun "I" by imitating the action of an adult. For instance, when helping to set the table an adult might say, "I am going to put the plate here." Then the child takes a turn saying, "I am going to put the cup here." In this activity a child is both cooperating with and imitating an adult.

There are two prerequisites that are necessary in order for a child to have an understanding of the context for using the pronoun "I". First, a child must be able to act independently, and second, a child must understand that other people act independently. David is an example of a child who is quite able to use "I" properly in nearly every context. He is a junior kindergarten child who is on the verge of playing cooperatively with other children. His present style of playing is usually referred to as "parallel play", which means that he is able to play along side other children in the same play space without interfering or playing with them. This shows that he is able to act independently. He is also aware that others act independently in that he

16

has become very interested in watching older children although he does not actually enter into their (cooperative) play.

David's mother spends a good deal of time interacting with him at home. He frequently helps her and she often spends time making things with him. It is through the opportunity to imitate his mother, while taking his own personal initiatives to make and do things that David has learned the skills necessary to use the pronoun "I".

Tanya is another kindergarten child who does not even parallel play. Unlike David, who can be directed and who can work with an adult, she is a very demanding individual. Her demands are not made with cooperation in mind. Typically, she takes toys away from other children by saying "me want this".

Tanya's behaviour seemed to stem from her relationship at home with her aunt who habitually gave in to her demands. She had discovered at a very early age a means to make her aunt compliant. To get her own way she wet herself instantly whenever her aunt did not respond to her demands.

Wetting herself was a strategy she tried out in the kindergarten class, but the teacher recognized it as a manipulation and refused to give in. She has not wet herself since although she continues to wet at home.

Given Tanya's inability to act in "parallel" or "cooperatively", it is not surprising that she does not display the ability to plan ahead. She always uses "me" in place of "I". Indeed, many would say that Tanya is egocentric. While Tanya may learn to parrot the pronoun "I" she may not grasp the full meaning including the cooperative characteristics of the pronoun. In all likelihood she will continue to have problems using "I" and "me" in the correct contexts.

On the other hand, it appears that David has learned perhaps by imitating his parents, how to initiate and plan activities. This difference in ability appears to be due to the cooperative relationship David has with his parents. He is beginning to carry this ability over into play and into his relationships with others in junior kindergarten. Since David's way of relating to others provides him with greater need to communicate with other children, he has more need for the pronoun "I" to initiate plans. Having more use for "I", he finds it easy to use when he is speaking. Clearly, David has developed an advantage over Tanya in the way that he communicates his intentions to others.

Characteristics of children using the (subjective) "I" versus "me" are

(i)  Can perform cooperative tasks with adults.

(ii) Shows an interest in the cooperative activites of other children (in many cases playing along-side other children while imitating them).

(iii) Plans activities *before carrying them out* as in "I am going to paint a house".

(iv) Initiates activities which call for the use of "I", such as "I want to climb on the slide with you".

The school is a place that gives children a new opportunity to transfer the behaviours learned in the family to the larger world of the classroom. The problems begin when some of the things that a child has already learned prove not to work in the new setting. Young children and many older children do not have the ability to stand back and take stock of whether or not their behaviour is appropriate. Often, if a behaviour works at home, it will be continued in nearly every new setting, even if it is inappropriate as a means of coping in the new setting. It is important for the teacher to have time set aside from kindergarten duties to observe the appropriateness of each child's coping style. Later, the teacher can work to selectively exclude behaviours that are immature or inappropriate, but first the teacher must become aware of these behaviours and how they may interfer with the child's potential to learn.

*Knowledge of own age:* By the time children are five they should be able to tell you their exact birthdate as well as their age. At three, most children have knowledge of their own age but they have memorized it in the same way that they know their name. Three-year olds do not understand the meaning of the number three in its cardinal sense, as can be shown by asking a three-year old, "How old were you last year?" or "How old will you be on your next birthday?" At age three many children will not understand that next year they will be one year older. As a result they have to relearn their age at the next birthday. This is not easy for them because they must have at least a beginning sense of cardinality. When you ask, "How old were you last year?" a four-year old *may* be able to hold up three fingers to indicate the right age.

*Verbal expression of emotions:* The pronoun "I" is also used to describe the child's feelings. "I am happy" and "I am sad," are two extremes of feelings which children can verbalize quite early. Beth Ann could use the pronoun "I" to express her feelings of being happy or sad when she was three; however, she was just learning to express the feeling of anger (being mad at someone) by the time she turned four. Children feel happy and sad before they have the ability to express these feelings in words. Before children can put a name to a feeling a child must be able to separate it from other feelings. Slowly, over a period of time children learn to differentiate each of their feelings as well as to learn new words to describe them.

Once a child is beginning to distinguish various moods, the words that are used to identify these moods need to be practiced. Adults can enhance such self-knowledge by using language to point to the mood of the child when the opportunity arises. Teachers of young children are often heard to make comments such as, "Joan's in a happy mood today" or "Does Mark feel sad today?" A good place to practise expressing moods is offered when reading favourite stories to children such as Jack and the Beanstalk. The reader will then be able to ask a child questions such as, "How do you think the Giant felt when he discovered that Jack had run off with the Golden Harp?" or "How do you think Jack's mother felt when Jack told her that he had the Giant's Golden Harp?" With older children the contrast in emotions brought about by the Golden Harp caper can be investigated by asking children, "How can the same thing cause one person to be happy and another person to be sad?"

*Knowledge of body parts and drawing a person:* The knowledge of body parts and the ability to include the body parts when drawing a person are quite related skills which should have begun to develop by the time a child is ready to enter junior kindergarten. In a child's development, the ability to draw often lags somewhat behind the naming of body parts. The drawings of three-year olds characteristically have only the head and body, or head with features only, even though they can easily point to six to ten body parts. The difference between naming and the child's drawing skills occurs partly because drawing requires a higher level of physical coordination, and also because the adult helps the child's naming by pointing to the drawing. The adult's pointing serves to sort the body into discrete parts, making the child aware that there are separate features to the body. Drawing also requires planning which means that a child must organize the features of a person on the page. By the time a child is five, all of the major body parts and facial features should be present and correctly organized in a drawing of a person.

*Assembling a puzzle of a person:* Between 4 and 4.5 years of age most children can assemble a jig-saw puzzle of a person. Although this task requires an organizational strategy, unlike the drawing, the parts are already present so the child can accomplish this task earlier.

Beth Ann, who is just four, placed the head first, next moved to the arms, but after that resorted to trial and error to organize the pieces. The strategies used to assemble a puzzle include the development of the ability to plan.

## Colour Concepts

1. 3 - 4 yr. – Using crayons the child can name 5 colours.
2. 3.5 - 4 yr. – Recognizing different shades of colour as being "more like" a given colour.
3. 4 - 5 yr. – Can name 8 colours.

## Size Concepts

4. 3 yr. – Understanding the concept "bigger".
5. 3 yr. – Understanding the concept "longer" and "shorter".
6. 3.5 - 5 yr. – Recognizing different shapes as being "more like" a given shape.

## Amount and Number Concepts

7. 2 yr. – Understands the concept "more".
8. 2 yr. – Can sort "one" block and "many".
9. 2 yr. – Can answer the question, "how old are you".
10. 3 yr. – Can count two blocks, saying, "One, two".
11. 3 yr. – Can count three objects, saying, "One, two, three."
12. 4 - 5 yr. – Can count 10 objects.
13. 4 - 5 yr. – Understands the concept of "pair". Gives two blocks.
14. 4 - 5 yr. – Understands the concept of "many". Gives more than two blocks.
15. 4 - 5 yr. – Understands the concept of "many". Gives more than five blocks.
16. 4 - 5 yr. – Understands the concept of "first" block in a row.
17. 4 - 5 yr. – Understands the concept of "last" block in a row.
18. 4 - 5 yr. – Understands the concept of "middle" block in a row.
19. 4 - 5 yr. – Understands the concept of "second" block in a row.
20. 4 - 5 yr. – Understands the concept of "how many?" The child is able to count 12 blocks.
21. 4 - 5 yr. – Understands the concept of "fewer".
22. 4 - 5 yr. – Rote counts to 30.

*Developing colour, shape and size concepts.* Developing the ability to discriminate among similar colours, shapes and sizes is crucial to similarity thinking. Teachers and parents who teach these concepts to young children can make collections of colour cards, shape cards and size cards which are very much alike rather than cards which are always identical. The intellectual benefit to the child is derived from performing exercises which call on the child to make similarity judgements.

In order to construct two-dimensional materials for "size" similarity exercises, an adult can cut out objects which look the same in every respect except for the size of objects. One such item may be selected as the target which can be placed in front of a child and used as the reference item from which to make comparisons. A child is handed one card at a time and asked, "Is it bigger?" (than the target). The child must decide whether it is bigger or smaller. The bigger cards are put into a pile on one side of the table. The smaller cards are placed in a pile on the other side of the table.

To make similarity judgements such as the size comparison task, a child must first notice that the card which is being compared to the target card is alike in every respect but one. Comparison of two objects, using only an attribute difference (e.g., size), can be made by children three to four years of age.

There are many variations on this exercise. For example, these exercises can be extended to comparisons of colour, shape and size. They are designed to direct a child's learning towards making decisions about relationships between objects. When children learn to make comparisons based on similarity relationships they are learning to generalize. The ability to generalize is central to the learning process. For example a child might be given eight objects, say, four apples and four horses. You would mix them up so that the apples and horses would not be in separate groups. In addition, you would choose apples that differed in size, shape and colour. You would also choose horses that differed in size, shape and colour. At this point you would give the child a simple instruction like, "show me the things that go together", or, following the format described above, you could put one horse and one apple apart from each other at the top of the display and ask the child to "find the ones that go here (pointing to the horse and apple in turn)". At least for adults, the apples are "most like" each other and the horses are "most like" each other, even though each apple and each horse is not exactly identical. The question for very young children is whether they also use similarity thinking to group objects together that have the same basic shapes but at the same time do not look exactly the same.

It is in this way that similarity thinking based on perceptual information leads to conceptual understanding, in this case that apples and horses no matter that the perceptual information is different, remain apples and horses. Children generalize from this to conclude that even though things might not look exactly the same, they may have a similar meaning. It is this kind of checking out of things to decide whether they are similar (in meaning) that gives rise to planning. Even the child who is just beginning to plan must attempt to get an "overview" of the situation or else there would not be a starting point. Similarity thinking makes it possible to develop an overview because many things are compared, even though they may not look exactly the same.

## Development of Planning Skills

1. 2.5 - 3 yr. – The child can put on coat, pants, ride a tricycle, climb stairs.
2. 3 yr. – Using blocks places one block "in front" of the other.
3. 3 yr. – Can place one block "behind" the other.
4. 3 yr. – Can dress completely and independently.
5. 3 - 4 yr. – Can draw a house in its entirety.
6. 3 - 4 yr. – Piling blocks to make something. After playing with the blocks putting them in any order, the child announces that the design looks like a "house" or some other object. Three- and four-year olds make these kinds of announcements after the fact.
7. 3 - 4 yr. – Solving a puzzle using only the pieces, without an outline framework. The child is required to assemble the pieces either horizontally or vertically.
8. 3 - 4 yr. – Assembling a jig-saw puzzle enclosed in a framework outlining the puzzle picture. The pieces must be inserted vertically and horizontally.
9. 5 yr. – The five-year-old can decide what he wants to build before starting to build. Statements like "Let's build a big alligator with the blocks" is typical of five-year olds planning their play.
10. 5 yr. – The child can use prepositions like "beside" and "next to" when giving directions to another child.

Some of the items in this list have been drawn from the Vulpé Assessment Battery (1969). Other items have been derived from discussions with kindergarten teachers.

The junior kindergarten teacher introduces many activities which will help the child learn to plan. By the time a child has finished senior kindergarten planning skills should be well established. A child should be able to tell you two or three moves in advance what he or she wants to accomplish. By questioning children about the moves that they plan to make, a teacher can decide just how well planning skills are developing.

Planning strategies are very difficult to learn because they require the child to use similarity thinking. It is only by understanding how things are similarly related that children are able to gain an overview of a situation so as to move from one idea to the next. There are two major approaches to helping young children learn planning strategies:

*Learning to make choices:* In the junior kindergarten room there are a number of activities from which to choose. A child can paint, use construction blocks, assemble puzzles, listen to stories, or listen to music. Children should be encouraged to choose their own activities. However, children often encounter difficulties that parents and teachers do not anticipate. For example, when children first start making choices, the number of these choices should be limited so that they are not overwhelmed. Children should be encouraged to stick with the chosen task for a reasonable period of time and not skip from one activity to another. To encourage planning, teachers should help children initiate, work at and conclude an activity before going on to another. On the other hand over a period of time children should be encouraged to play at a variety of activities. It is frequently the case that children feel more comfortable with activities that are familiar to them and prefer not to try something novel. Instead, they should be encouraged to take independent action, to try something different, because this will require them to plan out a new routine. The point here is that independence is necessary for planning, and that children should begin to exercise this kind of independence in kindergarten (see chapters five and seven).

*Organizing actvities:* Young children have trouble planning sequential tasks even when the task is well understood. In a task such as getting dressed, clothing has to be put on in a certain order. Since young children are not always aware of this order, they may choose the wrong item first. For instance, if mittens are put on first it is almost impossible to button or zipper a coat. Showing a child how to dress is one way of helping a child remember the correct sequence of dressing. Another way is to help children give an oral account of a dressing sequence that would work.

Learning to make choices and organizing tasks requires that the child understand how things are related. Similarity thinking makes it possible for the child to relate ideas to achieve an overview and hence to plan. As we have discussed in the previous chapter this is also the route to helping the child make generalizations – to transfer old learning to new situations. Since planning is a familiar term for teachers and since planning skills are practiced in junior kindergarten and kindergarten classes, we have introduced similarity thinking through the concept of planning. We hope to achieve a bridge between the old notion of planning and the new notion of similarity thinking. This is important because one is dependent upon the other. In other words, to practice similarity thinking is to practice planning. The demonstration of planning skills reflects the development of similarity thinking. The reader will get a more comprehensive look at similarity thinking in subsequent chapters.

## Kindergarten Preparation

The following questionnaire was designed for Beth Ann's parents although it could be modified for the parents of any child preparing to enter kindergarten. The questionnaire will sensitize the teacher to the individual needs of their students by taking into account the child's home experience.

Successful schooling is a cooperative affair. Cooperation does not imply that the teacher and the parent fulfill the same role since school is first and foremost a place where children learn to be independent. If children are to learn independence, they will learn best in a setting that takes into account their individual needs.

### Background

1. Exact age? . . . . . . . . . . . . . . . . . . . . . . . . . . . . . . .
2. Brothers? . . . . . . . . . . . . . . . . . . . . . . . . . . . . . . . .
   (a) Ages? . . . . . . . . . . . . . . . . . . . . . . . . . . . . . . . .
3. Sisters? . . . . . . . . . . . . . . . . . . . . . . . . . . . . . . . . .
   (a) Ages? . . . . . . . . . . . . . . . . . . . . . . . . . . . . . . . .
4. How long has she been at the present school? . . . . . . . . . . .
5. What school will she attend next? . . . . . . . . . . . . . . . . .
6. How old will she be when she goes to kindergarten? . . . . . . . .
7. Have you discussed kindergarten for Beth Ann with the school yet? . . . . . . . . . . . . . . . . . . . . . . . . . . . . . . . . . . . .

8. Who has looked after her in the afternoons? . . . . . . . . . . . .

9. What kind of activities does the nursery have you do at home? . .

10. How easily does she meet other people? . . . . . . . . . . . . . . .

11. What kind of group activities do they do with her at the present school? . . . . . . . . . . . . . . . . . . . . . . . . . . . . . . .

## Present Activity

12. What kind of activities does she prefer? – lego, crayons, dolls . . .

13. Do you read stories to her? . . . . . . . . . . . . . . . . . . . . . .

13. What are her favourite stories? . . . . . . . . . . . . . . . . . . . .

14. Does she like stories reread? . . . . . . . . . . . . . . . . . . . . .

14. Does she have favourite friends with whom she likes to play? . . .

15. What hours does her father work? . . . . . . . . . . . . . . . . . .

16. Does he have time to play with her? . . . . . . . . . . . . . . . . .

## Emancipation

17. How independent is she? . . . . . . . . . . . . . . . . . . . . . . .
    (a) feed herself? . . . . . . . . . . . . . . . . . . . . . . . . . . .
    (b) wash herself? . . . . . . . . . . . . . . . . . . . . . . . . . . .
    (c) brush her teeth? . . . . . . . . . . . . . . . . . . . . . . . . . .
    (d) dress herself? . . . . . . . . . . . . . . . . . . . . . . . . . . .
    (e) can she do up buttons? . . . . . . . . . . . . . . . . . . . . . .
    (f) can she do up zippers? . . . . . . . . . . . . . . . . . . . . . .
    (g) can she do up shoe laces? . . . . . . . . . . . . . . . . . . . . .

18. What are some things that she can do that we have not mentioned? . . . . . . . . . . . . . . . . . . . . . . . . . . . . . . . .

19. Does she have food preferences? What are they? . . . . . . . . . .

20. Will she try strange foods that she has not had before? . . . . . .

## Play

21. Does she play co-operatively (or parallel play)? . . . . . . . . . .

22. Can she play with another child without taking the other child's toys? . . . . . . . . . . . . . . . . . . . . . . . . . . . . . . . . . .

23. Can she play without physically hurting other children? . . . . . .

24. Can she follow instructions (one at a time)(two at a time)? . . . .
25. How long can she play with a toy at one time without losing interest? . . . . . . . . . . . . . . . . . . . . . . . . . . . . . . . . .
26. Does she play outside or inside? . . . . . . . . . . . . . . . . . . .
27. If she plays outside, what kinds of things does she like to do? . .
28. What kinds of things have you learned about children since you have had a Down's Syndrome child? . . . . . . . . . . . . . . . .
29. Looking back, how have you changed as parents from the time that Beth Ann was born? . . . . . . . . . . . . . . . . . . . . . . .

# Chapter 3

# Getting to Know the Child at Home

In chapter one we introduced the reader to Beth Ann who has Down's Syndrome. We observed Beth Ann at play as well as in the nursery school. We also assessed her for similarity thinking. The composite picture we provided begins to chronical her intellectual development as she turns four years of age. In chapter two we showed how teachers can become sensitized to individual needs like Beth Ann's by understanding the demands of kindergarten. In chapter three we discuss Andy, a kindergarten child who is not succeeding because of emotional adjustment problems. We suggest that emotional adjustment cannot be achieved independently of intellectual learning.

In the last chapter we mentioned that a co-operative effort between the home and school is essential if the child is to successfully adapt to the new and demanding expectations of the school. In this chapter we suggest that observing the child at home will help the teacher understand the individual needs and the strengths of the child. These observations will facilitate a positive transition from the home to the school. Often the child functions quite well, or at least with some measure of success at home and not so well at school. We suggest that more than incidental comments from parents are required to identify the individual needs and strengths of the child during this critical transition period.

What is necessary, in our view, is a systematic evaluation of home and school behaviour. The goal of this kind of evaluation would be to ensure that the strengths of home are transferred to school.

## Introducing Andy

Andy first arrived for senior kindergarten in early October, a month after the other children had started school. His parents had separated two years prior to this and during this time he had been living with his father and his grandparents. He was visited regularly by his mother for the first year, but since that time she had remarried and had stopped visiting him. In the first year of separation Andy's father had decided to work abroad in Saudi Arabia and the grandparents had assumed responsibility for raising Andy.

Subsequently the grandparents had elected not to send Andy to junior kindergarten and even in the second year there had been some reluctance about sending him to senior kindergarten. Other than his slightly small stature, Andy's only other distinguishing feature was his inordinately large blue eyes which were hidden most of the time by the fact that he usually hung his head. During his first three months in kindergarten he sat motionless for the most part, never participating with other children in the activities of the classroom.

## Observing Andy with His Grandparents

Andy's grandmother brought him to school each day and everyday he walked down the school hallway holding on tightly to her. As soon as he saw the kindergarten teacher or the teaching assistant he would quickly move to his grandmother's furthest hand so that he could hide behind her coat. While Andy was with his grandmother, he completely ignored the other children, and never spoke except to cry when his grandmother attempted to leave him alone in the classroom.

In this senior kindergarten classroom it is customary, when there are children who have difficulty adjusting, to encourage the parent to stay during the first few days. During this time Andy sat next to his grandmother's chair, with his head down, holding tightly onto her legs while the other children played and went about classroom routines. Whenever his grandmother attempted to leave, Andy would cry, very quietly and persistently, until she would relent and stay longer. The grandmother was clearly distressed about Andy's reaction to her leaving.

In the days following Andy's initial introduction to the classroom, the grandfather brought him to school and explained to the teacher that his wife found the ordeal much too stressful. At first when he arrived in the morning he also stayed for a short period of time. He did not allow the child to physically hold onto him as the grandmother had. Instead, when he arrived, he took off Andy's coat and hat and placed him on the rug with the other children. During this time Andy became quite introverted, sitting quietly while the other children played around him.

Eventually the grandfather requested an interview with the teacher. He told her that in his opinion Andy was "doing just fine" and that he was not prepared to stay in the classroom any longer. The teacher agreed since his presence in the classroom did not seem to be helping Andy cope. On the following morning the grandfather delivered Andy to the classroom but did not remain.

## Andy's Adjustment to the Classroom

Andy simply stood where his grandfather had left him until the teacher took him by the hand and led him to the cloak hall. He did not fuss or cry, but stood looking downward. After she took his coat he sat quietly on the bench until he was led by the hand to sit with the other children on the rug. During the next few days he showed no interest in the toys or the children but sat passively watching the other children play. When another child would approach him he would show no sign of recognition but instead would turn his head as if to watch something else in the room. Occasionally, some of the children would approach him and try to engage him in play. When this happened he would pull away making a whimpering sound.

Initially the teacher allowed him time to adjust to the newness of the classroom. She said she felt that it might take him some time to become acquainted with the children and the activities, but perhaps he would shortly begin to show an interest in the kindergarten. When time passed and she saw that Andy was not adjusting in the usual manner, she tried to intervene by taking him to the activities. While he showed no reluctance to follow the teacher, he did not participate and ignored the active play of the others.

## An Interview with the Grandparents

After some time had passed and Andy was still not participating in any of the classroom activities, the teacher invited the grandparents to return for another interview. During the interview the grandmother cried frequently. She said she felt that she was not doing the right thing by leaving the boy all by himself when he was so unhappy. She felt that he was an innocent victim in the marriage breakup and that as a result he required more comforting than other children. She related stories about how happy he was at home when he worked and played with her in the kitchen in contrast to his unhappiness at school.

Andy's grandfather was not particularly sympathetic to the goals of the kindergarten. He said he felt that the kindergarten class was far too noisy for children to learn and that the children should not be allowed to walk freely around in the classroom. He added that he felt there was nothing wrong with Andy. Andy's quietness in the class-room merely indicated that he was a well-behaved boy.

His grandmother claimed that Andy spoke to her a great deal at home and frequently stayed with her when she was working in the kitchen, setting the table and helping with the dishes. She had with her a number of drawings which she said he had done at home. From the teacher's perspective these drawings looked quite good.


## Entries from the Teacher's Journal

November 5 – Andy had been placed with a small group of children who were playing in the kitchen area. He was sitting at the table near the other children but not participating. When I went over to see what was happening with the group, I noticed that he had wet himself. He must be taken to the washroom at regular intervals.

November 8 – After coming in from the playground Andy was undressed by the assistant along with the other children. When the others were called to the circle Andy was somehow overlooked. He sat for nearly thirty minutes before someone noticed that he was not with us. When taken by the hand and led, he was reluctant to come to the circle.

November 12 – When I tried to get Andy to put a shape in a puzzle he turned his head and let his hand go quite limp.

November 13 – The children want Andy to sit nearby when they are playing. Sometimes when I placed him in the kitchen center they set a place at the table for him. He never seems to acknowledge this activity.

November 14 – When Andy was sitting in the circle today at snack time, one of the children tried to feed him a piece of orange. He made a face and turned his head back and forth to avoid taking it into his mouth. She was so persistent in offering him the orange that she finally managed to get it into his mouth. He immediately spit out the orange.

*In the playground.* Andy does not like to go out of doors. Even on bright sunny days when he is warmly dressed he stands where he is placed in the playground and shivers until he is returned indoors. On a number of occasions the teacher tried to get him to participate in activities by placing him in a wagon. Each time he stiffened so much that it was impossible to keep him from falling off and hurting himself.

*The psychologist.* The school psychologist visited the classroom on several occasions to observe Andy. In his report he noted that he was quite baffled by this case, since "the passivity of the child prevents useful observations and also makes testing procedures impossible to carry out."

## The First Breakthrough

The first indication that progress could be made with Andy in the classroom happened when the itinerant music teacher visited the room bringing with her a group of instruments including a xylophone. She taught the lesson near Andy who was sitting on the rug with a small group. While the children were absorbed with the task of working out their own rhythms on the percussion instruments, the assistant noticed that Andy's face expressed intense interest.

When the music session ended, Andy's teacher discussed the assistant's observation with the music teacher, noting particularly the interest that the percussion instruments seemed to have generated. She asked the music teacher to try out some percussion sounds with him. The music teacher brought over two xylophones. She placed one in front of Andy and the other in front of herself.

Initially, Andy averted his eyes from the music teacher and her instrument. However as the teacher began experimenting with a few notes, he lifted his head, smiled very slightly, and began watching the xylophone. The music teacher repeated the note that had first drawn Andy's attention. At this point, Andy's hand was being held by the teacher. He did not let it go limp but rather held onto the hammer as the teacher struck the note.

Andy was encouraged to hold the hammer directly over the note that was so compelling so that his teacher could let go of his hand. Andy seemed to enjoy this and with the help of the teacher hit the note several times.

On the following day the teacher placed the hammer on the xylophone directly in front of Andy. Although he did not immediately begin to play the instrument, he began to make eye contact with the teacher for the first time. He looked directly at the teacher and after catching her eye, looked down at the xylophone.

The teacher was delighted with this new response. The day following this breakthrough each time she passed by Andy, she would help him play the instrument. Initially he would repeat the note that he had originally found so attractive, stiffening whenever the teacher tried to hold his hand over another part of the keyboard. However,

31

over a period of time she discovered that he was willing to experiment with other notes that were immediately adjacent. Finally, on the fourth day, Andy voluntarily picked up the hammer and experimented on his own.

## The Second Interview with Andy's Grandmother

With the good news of Andy's progress, his grandmother was delighted to come for another interview. This time the grandfather did not attend. During this interview Andy's grandmother revealed that Andy had a toy xylophone at home which he often played. She also related that he had a favourite stuffed bear that he insisted she read the same stories to each night at bedtime. He would always listen attentively as she read these stories to the bear.

## Bridging the Gap with Similar Experiences

As a result of the success arising from the discovery of Andy's interest in the xylophone, the teacher decided to try to bridge the gap between more home and school activities. Andy's grandmother made a tape-recording of his favourite stories which could be brought to school and played. The teacher took advantage of the recording to introduce Andy to the listening center. She sat him at the table with headphones on and placed his favourite story book in front of him. A look of amazement came over his face when he heard his grandmother's voice relating the story. For the first few listening sessions the teaching assistant helped him turn the pages of the book to keep up with the story, but very quickly he was able to take on this task by himself.

Over the remaining months that Andy was in the kindergarten class the teacher was able to introduce numerous activities that brought home and school experiences together. While Andy never did become a gregarious or talkative individual at school this bridging technique helped him adjust in large measure to school experience.

## The Similarities Experience as a Strategy

There are children in every kindergarten class that exhibit Andy's behaviour to a certain extent. There is also evidence that similarities experience to bring home and school together, can be successful with many children. In a recent public address given in Toronto, the

32

renowned violinist Yehudi Menuhin described a technique successful with autistic children which was not unlike the one used with Andy. He described clinical sessions conducted by music therapists, in which the therapist with the aid of a musical instrument would mimic the sounds made by autistic children. The therapist would use a single sound gradually working up a sympathetic communication between the two of them and consequently breaking down the child's wall of isolation. As communication increased between the therapist and the child, the single sound would be supplemented by the introduction of additional sounds of relative similarity. In this approach we see movement from the familiar to the unfamiliar. The child begins to take risks in learning as well as increasing communication with others.

## The Key is Familiarity

The child at home or at play obviously has the desire to initiate activities of one kind or another and feels good about those activities. Our purpose in this book is to suggest that children might do similar kinds of things when they are first introduced to school. In this way school becomes familiar and the bonus is that the child feels secure. By emphasizing the familiar and the transfer of similar things from home to school, the child's feelings of insecurity are lessened and never become the focus of school activities.

Insecurity should not be treated independently of mainstream classroom learning activities. Therapy or self concept enhancement sessions should not be attempted in isolation. Instead, these sessions can be replaced or supplemented by similarities training showing the child how the familiar activities of home can be found at school. The reassurance and feelings of security the child experiences in this kind of introduction to school life establishes the "emotional" ground from which the child is able to reach out to new experience. The relationship between the emotionality of the child and the child's developing learning strategies are explored in more detail in chapter seven.

---

*Activities challenge the child's learning potential*

Student teachers in preservice training courses are rarely aware of the relationship that exists between successful learning and feelings of self-esteem. When they are assigned to tutor a student who is having problems learning they soon discover that failure is often accompanied by feelings of personal inadequacy. The temptation is to treat the feelings of low esteem independently of the cause – an inability to deal adequately with learning tasks. The child will not feel inadequate when learning is no longer a problem. Pats on the back to comfort the child are not good enough.

## Personal Efficacy

While the teacher exercises control over the learning situation, the actual act of learning is up to the child. Learning in school largely depends upon how the child views the learning process itself. If the child does not regard the task of learning as a desirable one then very little learning will take place. But curiosity and learning are natural human endeavours and under most circumstances when curiosity is aroused it is difficult to keep children from learning. Difficulty arises when we wish to prescribe that certain things are to be learned. In this case the initiative may not come from the child and curiosity is not aroused. Furthermore, the child may show resistance to learning in the face of the unfamiliar. The things that we intend children to learn are not always within the framework of their secure experiences. Lack of familiarity may cause children to begin to avoid the very tasks that we want them to learn. *We believe that familarity leads to curiosity which, in turn, leads to learning and to feelings of security.*

It is not obvious how some children come to acquire the ability to be effective learners while others do not. It would seem to most

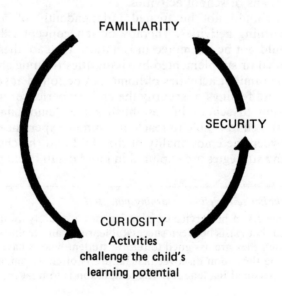

FAMILIARITY

SECURITY

CURIOSITY
**Activities
challenge the child's
learning potential**

observers of active kindergarten children at play that curiosity and learning are natural human endeavours. However the fragile nature of these young personalities becomes apparent under some circumstances.

Fleming (1978) investigated a group of eight-year olds from working-class families and found that they were much more fluent when talking to other children about solving a problem than when they talked to the teacher. One way of understanding working-class children's difficulty in talking to the teacher about problem solving is to examine the nature of their personal security. In this case it would seem that these children are not as secure about dealing with the teacher as they are with the other children. According to William Blatz (1944), personal security is bound to their experiences. Working-class children often have little experience outside school with teachers but a great deal of experience with other children like themselves. Consequently they experience a certain anxiety when addressing teachers because the teaching role is unfamiliar.

Personal security which is bound to particular circumstances Blatz called dependent security. Someone else assumes responsibility for the actions of the child and consequently the child experiences feelings of anxiety when that person is not present (see chapter seven for a discussion of Blatz's theory).

This explanation certainly could account for Andy's anxiety in the kindergarten. It appears that he was totally dependent upon his grandmother and the unfamiliar circumstances of the kindergarten did not stimulate feelings of comfort and security in him. The most difficult aspect of dependent security is that the individual is forced to rely upon familiar places and faces to get along in the world. This is the reason school can be so important for children. They learn how to deal in some degree with the unfamiliar, and acquire some flexibility in novel circumstances.

## Learning to Deal with the Novel

Carol Davis (1966) used the concept of emancipation (the growth of individual independence) as the guiding principle in analyzing the development of seven children, studied over a period of twenty years at the Institute of Child Study. Davis, in *Room to Grow*, used Blatz's security theory to examine the role that personal security played in developing the independence of these children.

The important point about emancipation is that the child progressively learns to deal with novel situations. The value of school is that it is a novel situation which is structured to allow children to encounter the new, within a controlled, safe framework. School experiences should eventually prepare children to live in an unpredictable adult world.

As can be seen in the case study of Andy, learning to deal with the novel is best accomplished initially by bridging between the home and the school. It should be noted however that for bridging to be most successful for the development of independent security, the teacher should progressively move the child towards dealing effectively with what is novel in school experiences.

In order to become an effective, secure learner, within the framework of the school, Andy's experiences with his musical instrument at home was of paramount importance. Adapting the familiar experience of his music to the novelty of the school provided a secure reference point around which to organize the other novel experiences of kindergarten.

Not all home experiences were of equal value in helping Andy adapt to the school. In fact, those home experiences which required the continued presence of his grandmother in the kindergarten were detrimental to Andy's adaptation to school. It would be equally unacceptable for a child who used "baby-talk" to continue to practise it without the school making efforts to remediate this behaviour. The purpose of "bridging" is to selectively bring into the new situation only those experiences which have the potential to enhance the child's ability to learn to deal with the novel.

Children attain a state of *mature dependent security* when they acquire a reciprocal dependency with those in the school who have mutual needs. Trust and familiarity are the vehicles for helping a child attain this level of security. When children become dependently secure they have a foundation from which to reach out to new experience. The ultimate aim of providing new experience is to guide children in such a way that they attain *independent security* which can be achieved only through learning (Blatz, 1944). This results in the strange becoming familiar which in turn leads to new learning. This kind of learning requires greater risk.

Andy will make an important breakthrough when he can abandon the familiar, take up novel tasks, and discover that the new skills he learns will help him to better cope with new situations. He will eventually accept the feelings of insecurity that come with new learning and translate these feelings into curiosity, thereby becoming an independently secure individual (see chapter seven for an extended treatment of these ideas).

36

# Chapter 4

# Two Seven-Year Olds Talk About Rain

In this chapter we introduce two children who are asked to explain how it rains. An interesting paradox emerges in that one child, who seemingly gives childish explanations, may really be more advanced in her use of similarity thinking than another child who is more adult-like in his explanations. When first listening to Georgia's account, an adult is delighted with the "childishness" of the response but at the same time may dismiss it as simply being incorrect. On the other hand, Herbert's explanation is deceptively impressive (definitely not childish) because his elaborate vocabulary suggests that he understands the concepts whereas in actual fact he does not. By analyzing these children's comments using the model of similarity thinking we come to understand two things, first, the kind of thinking that a child is using and second, what this way of thinking implies for the child's emotional development. We conclude the chapter by showing how similarity thinking can be exercised to help children become independently secure learners so as to realize their potential to learn.

## Georgia and Herbert Talk about Rain

Several years ago while on a field trip, we were forced to seek shelter from a sudden shower. This can spell disaster for an outing. However on this day, the shelter took the form of a deserted barn which was interesting on its own. We made ourselves comfortable and waited for the storm to clear.

Some of the children became restless and fearful, so we began to talk about the storm and why it rains. Georgia, who was seven years old at the time, was quick to share her observations and her reasoning about how it rains. For Georgia it rains, "When the clouds get full of water; they bump together and the rain falls or it just comes out." When asked what causes them to bump together she answered, "They might be passing by and they just bump because they don't have eyes."

When first listening to Georgia's account, an adult is tempted to be delighted with the childishness of the response but at the same time dismiss it as simply being incorrect. We suggest throughout this book that the reader should recognize these seemingly inaccurate accounts as necessary steps in the development of mature thinking. In fact, we will attempt to convince the reader that the later forms of more mature thinking are founded upon earlier forms; that evidence of earlier thinking continue to be present in the thinking of older children. In chapter six the development of similarity thinking is described in some detail to help the reader understand how children's reasoning changes over time.

Clouds present a particular difficulty for children. Unlike other objects that are within reach, clouds are not readily accessible. They seem to just float across the sky, never appearing again in exactly the same form. When Georgia was asked, "How do clouds move?" she responded, "I don't exactly know but I think when there is a tiny breeze in the sky, they just flow along in the sky. Sometimes they make pictures when the wind blows on a certain side."

Deprived of an opportunity to know clouds intimately, Georgia must depend upon her observations and try to make as much sense out of them as she can. For instance, when she was asked to talk about cloud movement she said, "Clouds move in the sky. When I was sitting in a chair outside in the back garden there was a cloud in the sky. It was right above my head and then I looked up and it was gone."

She had made an excellent observation, but when she was asked where the clouds might go, she appeared baffled and replied, "Anywhere in the sky. They are not headed anywhere in the sky. They just go around in the sky."

Like navigators prior to Christopher Columbus, Georgia has no notion of a world beyond the horizon. She does not have ready explanations for what she cannot perceive.

## Georgia Searches for Answers She Can Understand

Since Georgia is only seven years of age, her thinking is largely confined to what she can see and touch. Therefore the best way that she can understand "how it rains" is for her to describe it in terms of something she already knows and understands. That is why she chose to describe clouds as "... soft stuff like cotton floating and they just bump together and the water just pours out everywhere. Because they look like cotton batton because it looks like that."

It is interesting to note that Georgia's choice of similarities discloses just how she thinks about this problem. She depends very much on what is familiar in her past experience. Because she notices that clouds look like they have the qualities of cotton, she likens cloud to cotton. A cloud must act like cotton since clouds and cotton, look alike.

Since she cannot conceive of a cloud as "a condensed watery vapour", she thinks that a cloud must be composed of material more substantial in nature and therefore much like cotton. She also knows that clouds are "soft-stuff" and that even a "tiny breeze in the sky" is sufficient to "make pictures when the wind blows on a certain side".

For Georgia, the visual resemblance between clouds and cotton means that a cloud will absorb water in the same manner as cotton. It must also follow, that if a cloud absorbs water like cotton, it must also release it in the same manner when it is compressed. According to Georgia's reasoning, when two clouds bump together they will be compressed like cotton, causing the water to pour out everywhere as rain. Her reasoning relies on familiarity. Since Georgia is most familiar with her own body, she compares the movement and action of clouds to people. This is very evident when she says that clouds bump together because they do not have eyes. To Georgia, the clouds seem to have almost human qualities, moving across the sky seeming to have purpose to their movement.

## Georgia's Advanced Reasoning

When Georgia was asked how the water gets into the clouds she showed evidence of a high level of reasoning when she replied, "It's like how does dew get on the grass. I don't know how dew gets on the grass but the moisture gets on the grass ... the moisture gets in the clouds and makes water." In this response she shows that she is approaching, but has not yet achieved, the kind of thinking that eleven and twelve year old children can use. Her statements are very close to the hypothetical (or what if) thinking engaged in by adolescents. Like hypothetical thinkers she makes two statements which compare similar processes. Unlike hypothetical thinkers she does not continue to examine the phenomenon; she is satisfied with her answer.

Hypothetical thinking develops with maturation as Piaget has demonstrated in numerous studies. However this way of thinking does require practice. Clearly Georgia's thinking is on the verge of a more advanced kind of thought. Hypothetical thinking will increase her ability to consider alternatives when she encounters novel problems. This kind of thinking can be encouraged through modeling, by someone who already has the ability to think in this manner.

## The Risk in Reasoning

There is a great deal of risk in learning to consider alternatives because there is much uncertainty in learning something new. The learner is confronted with questions that do not have ready-made answers and speculation becomes an important part of finding ways to answer the questions. This is a very vulnerable position for children, because they are open to ridicule if they answer in a way that others find difficult to accept. For instance, near the end of the conversation Georgia was asked again where rain comes from. She replied, "Maybe the clouds get too full of water and when it bumps the water goes to one end of the cloud." To someone who thinks more scientifically this answer is absurd. The temptation is to point out to the child the absurdity of the answer rather than to teach the child how to explore the idea to a different kind of conclusion.

Adults frequently find it difficult,in the face of seemingly absurd ideas, to contain the urge to tell children that their answers are blatantly wrong. However, it is really important that they suppress this urge because they can easily prevent neophyte scientists like Georgia from discussing their thoughts openly with others. Discerning parents realize that for first thoughts to blossom, they must be nurtured by careful listening. What young children say provides only a glimpse into their present understanding and only vaguely suggests what that understanding will become.

## Herbert Talks about Rain

On the occasion of the storm, Herbert, who was also seven, offered a different explanation about how it rains. He appeared to disapprove of Georgia's version and said. "The rain comes out of the clouds. I am not sure how this is done, but it has to get into the clouds. The water that gets into the clouds comes out of either the lakes or the oceans as vapour into the clouds. Too much of it comes into the clouds and they cannot hold it all and it comes down as rain."

It is interesting to note that when most adults first hear Herbert's explanations they find it much more impressive than Georgia's. When asked why they find his description better they usually cite his vocabulary, particularly his use of the word "vapour". They are impressed that such a young child even has the word in his vocabulary.

His teacher, also impressed by his vocabulary, asked him what he meant by vapour and he answered, "Vapour is where water gets hot like in a kettle. All the water molecules start moving very fast and some changes begin to happen in the water. And it goes up as vapour which is sometimes called steam."

Herbert's definition of vapour would certainly indicate a profound knowledge of the term. To make absolutely sure of his knowledge, he was asked how steam differed from vapour and he replied, "It is the same." While this is not strictly true, one would not expect a seven-year old to be able to differentiate between steam and vapour. In his description he presents an amazing amount of knowledge, much more than we would expect from a child his age. Nevertheless his teacher pursued the difference by enquiring whether vapour is necessarily "hot". Herbert answered, "Usually if it comes out of a kettle it is, but in a cloud it is usually kind of cool. Vapour is tiny little drops of water, so tiny that they are light, and everyone knows that heat rises and those little tiny drops of water get hot. They rise and when they rise out of your kettle they appear as some kind of white stuff."

A new tact was tried by asking him what makes the vapour white. He said rather emphatically, "I don't have any idea."

## Understanding Herbert's Argument

In many ways Herbert's thinking is not what it would seem. Initially one's attention is drawn to his use and description of words like "vapour" and "molecule". However, these facts obscure the similarities between the two children. In Herbert's first description he says that "too much of it comes into the clouds and the clouds cannot hold it all and it come down as rain." In spite of the elaborate vocabulary, he seems to really understand the cloud to be like a large vessel which gradually fills up until it can hold no more water. When the cloud can hold no more, the excess comes down as rain. If this explanation of Herbert's thinking about rain is accurate, then it seems difficult to account for his apparently excellent description of the action of molecules which is the cause of evaporation. There seems to be an inconsistency in Herbert's thinking. Unquestionably, he possesses the ability to learn, in that he can talk about difficult factual academic material. Unfortunately, however, his information is derived from someone else's understanding.

Indeed, early on, Herbert had displayed an amazing capacity to remember facts. His parents prized his ability to remember quite complex ideas and spent time teaching and encouraging him to do so. Consequently, much of his self esteem came to depend upon his capacity to accurately convey bits and pieces of knowledge. The problem was that the ideas that he learned were not his. In fact, he had only a superficial notion of many of the ideas that he discussed, although he almost invariably was able to talk about these ideas in an appropriate context.

An inspection of his explanation about "how it rains" shows that he did not try out one unique idea of his own. Every idea that he presented had been considered before, probably in family discussions where the "correct" answers were provided. This is particularly evident when he was asked the one question that he had not anticipated, "What makes vapour white?" His refusal to answer unexpected questions was very typical of his mode of responding. In fact, novel situations created such a dilemma for Herbert that he was often prevented from completing even minor tasks such as printing a single word.

Georgia, on the other hand, was brought up in a household where every idea was of interest. She was encouraged to explore new ideas. Instead of contradicting her "childish" thoughts, she was encouraged to take these ideas further along. Georgia's thinking was very acceptable to herself while Herbert always relied on the approval of adults. Consequently, Georgia was able to speculate on many possible answers. When a problem was posed, she would attempt to use her own resources to solve it, frequently relating them to familiar situations. This clearly helped her realize more of her learning potential. Herbert, on the other hand, depended upon second-hand knowledge, as is evident in this statement, "Everyone knows that heat rises."

# Listening to Children's Thinking

The most important thing an adult can do is to help children think about their experiences. This not only helps children focus their thoughts so that they become more effective problem solvers but it also helps them to become less dependent individuals. The world becomes a more predictable place when children are equipped to use experiences that they already understand to make sense out of the novel events in their lives.

As can be seen in Herbert's case, the adults in his life did not accept his thinking as valid, but instead, encouraged him to borrow "answers" from others. This is because many adults judge the correctness of children's thoughts according to an adult standard; the way they believe children should think. This can lead to an emphasis on the correctness of the answer which clearly in Herbert's case resulted in his borrowing knowledge from others.

It is difficult for children to borrow knowledge from adults since they frequently do not understand the reasoning upon which the knowledge is based, nor do they have the experience to put the knowledge into an understandable context. If children are to understand the things that we teach them, they must be helped to acquire strategies for thinking about their own experiences, those that have occurred in the past and those that may occur in the future.

Solving novel problems that have meaning in terms of personal experience can serve to help children gain a greater sense of security because they will no longer have to depend upon someone else to interpret their experiences for them. They will become independent thinkers and over a period of time independent thinking becomes a habit, a way of life that leads to feelings of security in adulthood. However, becoming an independently secure thinker is like becoming an independently secure swimmer; skills need to be exercised. In order to gain the most from exercise, it is necessary to have a schedule of exercises that are appropriate.


## Exercising Similarity Thinking

Similarity thinking can be exercised to help children like Georgia and Herbert become independently secure learners. The model of similarity thinking describes seven distinct types of thinking. In this chapter we help to make them more easily understood by dividing the seven types of thinking into three major divisions: a) analysis/synthesis: convergent thinking, b) overview/"big picture": holistic thinking and c) imagination/creativity: divergent thinking.

In the first major kind of thinking, children understand their experiences by comparing things that they can observe directly. They use a combination of analysis-pulling things apart and synthesis-putting things together – mental operations that form the basis of "most like" and completely alike judgements. One of the most important characteristics of this first division of thinking is that children must be able to make direct observations of their experience before they are able to think about this experience. Therefore those features of things that are pulled apart and put back together in similarity comparisons must

43

be observable. In the case of the blind child, direct experience is obtained through a combination of touch, taste and hearing.

The second major division of similarity thinking relies on more indirect methods of observation. This can be achieved when children use particular kinds of thinking, like analogical thinking, to come to conclusions that are not based on their direct observations but rather conclusions that come about as the result of conceptual analysis. Other indirect methods of observation involve using instruments like telescopes or microscopes to make experiences available that would be quite impossible with the unaided eye. In education, indirect methods of observation include making inferences and reading between the lines of written prose. Children are able to do this in our view, by using "overview" similarity thinking. Overview thinking makes it possible for the child to consider the "big picture" in order to understand how the smaller parts make sense in the larger scheme of things. One can see this when the child uses a jig-saw puzzle picture to make sense of the puzzle parts. The parts take on a new meaning as they become integrated into the whole picture. Overview thinking also makes use of information that comes out of indirect methods of observation. We see this when children begin to plan how to achieve goals even when they may not have experienced those goals beforehand. For example, they would have to imagine that reading between the lines will tell them something that they did not understand before.

In order to plan, children must consider the *means* necessary to achieve a goal. For example, overview thinking gives rise to planning when children consider the steps (derived through analysis) in relation to the goal. We see this when children start to plan where to begin to put the pieces together in a jig-saw puzzle. Remember Beth Ann began with the head because it was most familiar to her. As similarity thinking develops, children will consider more of the "big-picture" and become more deliberate and systematic in their planning; able to reflect upon more than one possible course of action. As suggested above, children begin to set goals even when these goals may not have been experienced before. This takes us to the third major division of the seven types of similarity thinking.

The third kind of similarity thinking makes it possible for the child to use divergent thinking, for example, to consider alternate means to solve problems as well as to notice that there is a problem in the first place. These thinking skills allow children to use imagination and creativity in their plans for achieving goals and solving problems. For example children are able to come up with new questions and problems that they want to solve on their own. Young children will often

44

innovate on the rules of a game. Sometimes they will even invent a new one.

It is important to note that overview thinking skills are "pivotal" in the sense that they are used with convergent similarity thinking (Thinking 1-4) as well as with divergent similarity thinking (Thinking 6-7). This is why overview thinking is described as Thinking 5, to suggest that it works with both convergent and divergent types of thinking. Children, even before they enter junior kindergarten and certainly by the time they enter senior kindergarten, are beginning to develop overview thinking skills. These skills continue to develop through adolescence. The important point is that very young children can use overview thinking to co-ordinate both convergent and divergent thinking in their planning even though their ability to do this is at a rudimentary stage of development. For example, the three- or four-year old may re-name something – a blanket over two chairs becomes a house – but this is not done in a reflective or deliberate way. An eleven- or twelve-year old may deliberately use an analogy (Thinking 4) or a metaphor (Thinking 7) to compare different things like blankets and chairs in order to come away with a new understanding of both of these things; that in combination they can represent or stand for something different, in this case a house. For example, blanket: chair as roof (of a house): walls (of a house).

The reader may wish to go beyond this very general introduction to similarity thinking. Chapter 6 provides a detailed description of the model by showing how it is used as an assessment instrument. Our purpose in giving a general introduction in this chapter is to provide additional insight into the behaviour of Georgia and Herbert. Herbert seems to be using overview thinking skills with convergent thinking but not in a very successful way with divergent thinking. Even Herbert's convergent thinking is not what it should be, possibly because he is not learning for himself. He is regurgitating answers someone else has given him. Georgia, on the other hand, is clearly experimenting with divergent thinking. This gives her responses a child-like character. However she is learning for herself. Consequently, Georgia is exercising her potential to learn more completely than Herbert. In the next chapter we suggest an instructional format that will exercise both convergent and divergent thinking skills. In the remainder of this chapter we make the point that Herbert may be suffering from a "crisis of confidence". Thinking exercises will have no effect until this emotional blockage is overcome. Interestingly, Georgia may also experience a crisis of confidence. This will happen if her explorations into divergent thinking are constantly put down as being childish. Georgia's example should make it abundantly clear how important it

45

is to understand the child's developing thinking skills and in particular the development of similarity thinking. We want to applaud Georgia's excursions into divergent thinking. We want to encourage her to practice coordinating overview thinking with both convergent and divergent thinking. She needs practice planning, using both of these major types of similarity thinking. When Georgia gets this kind of support, affecting both her emotionality and her developing thinking skills, she will be exercising the full range of her potential to learn.

## Crisis of Confidence

Learning skills and confidence are two different sides of the same coin and one side of the coin does not have much meaning without the other. Children who have problems learning, most often only show one side of the learning skills/confidence coin. For that very reason, many people become caught in the trap of only dealing with one aspect of the learning problem at a time while ignoring the other. Like the value of coinage, both faces must appear if the coin is to retain its value. Secure feelings about our ability to learn depend upon the development of learning skills as well as upon the development of confidence. It is the interaction between these two sides of the learning potential coin that allows us to venture forth and acquire knowledge.

A child enters the world in a state of *dependent security* (Blatz, 1944). This means that in the early years, adults not only make the decisions for a child but also accept the consequences for the child's actions. For instance, while shopping in a store, parents frequently ride their children in grocery carts. Whenever a very young child comes close to the food stacks, they usually reach out and help themselves to whatever is on the shelves. For the most part, parents accept responsibility for the child's actions by retrieving the items and replacing them on the shelves.

When parents assume responsibility for their children in many different situations throughout the day, they provide them with a sense of security. Children are dependently secure when they are very young since they ultimately rely on their parents to accept the consequences for their actions. From the child's point of view it is satisfying when someone else accepts these consequences for them. As adults, we acknowledge that young children are not yet old enough to assume responsibility for their actions.

When an adult remains extremely dependent we term the behaviour "childish". This behaviour is characterized by an individual acting in accordance with selfish desires without considering the needs of others. But everyone remains dependent upon others, in some manner, for some things. For instance, we learn to depend upon such things as immunization, social position and money.

Dependent security can be such a comfortable state that it is amazing that we ever make the effort to emerge from it. However, children from the very first, act purposely to achieve their own ends. Whether they do this in a dependent or an independent fashion largely depends upon their early learning experiences. Many well intentioned parents become so overly protective that their children never truly become independent. Instead these children simply learn to exchange one form of dependency for another throughout their lifetime. Children themselves may encourage continued dependency. For example a child may have had a traumatic experience that reduces his or her desire to take risks. Consider the possible consequences for a child who is riding a tricycle too close to a stairwell and experiences a nasty fall on the stairs. The experience may make the child reluctant to use the tricycle again.

To a large extent, whether or not the child is able to take further independent action depends upon the way the incident is treated by the parents. Children are very resilient and usually after a brief recovery interval they want to venture forth again.

These kinds of experiences are valuable for teaching children that the consequences of their actions are both physical and social. The *physical consequences* of an action are immediate and real. In the case of the child who approached too close to the stairwell the fall and the resulting abrasions from the fall are physical consequences. There are *social consequences* to the fall as well. These are the reactions of the adults. Not only do children learn quickly from the experience itself, but they also learn to "read" the adult's emotional responses. From the adult's (or in some cases sibling's) response, they take their cue about how to react in the future.

A child builds a pattern of dependency or one of independence early in life. Subsequently, when parents are not present, when for example children first go to school, each child may experience insecurity to a different degree. At this point the child makes a decision about how the new experience is to be handled. The child has one of three courses to choose from and the choice will depend upon his or her ability to accept risks:

1. *The withdrawal to family dependency option*: The child withdraws from solving his own problems in school or elsewhere and returns to a previously satisfactory behaviour where someone else can accept

the consequences for his or her actions. An example is depending upon the parent for organizing simple activities such as looking after one's personal hygiene and keeping track of one's belongings.

2. *Acting through an adopted dependency option*: The adopted dependency can be to a person or a thing. Children can transfer their attachment from the immediate family to an aunt, grandmother or teacher.

3. *The aggressive problem-solving option*: In this option the child sees the advantage of making an effort to problem solve. The child is willing to take risks witout fearing the physical or social consequences.

The last option is the most productive for the child since a positive relationship is developed between learning and emotional security. These ideas are discussed more fully in chapter seven.

There is a strong possibility that Herbert's inability to solve problems is based on his feelings of insecurity since he has apparently adopted the family dependency option. He has convergent learning skills as can be seen in his excellent use of words. What he cannot do very well is verify his knowledge by checking "the facts" against his personal observations. His lack of personal security, does not allow him to accept the validity of his own observations.

It might seem unbelievable that Herbert would choose the dependency option which would obviously handicap him. However his attachment to the family is very real. Consequently, it is difficult for him to consider other responses to potential learning situations.

According to William Blatz,

> ... he acquires many of the tastes, prejudices, and customs of the family, and develops a degree of loyalty depending upon his faith in the individuals and their judgement ... Certain artificial factors serve as symbols for his dependent experience – his name, his home, his immediate possessions, such as his cup, spoon, bed, clothes, etc. (Blatz, 1944, p. 183)

It should be noted that Herbert's problems have their basis in a choice that he made as a result of his early home experiences. His choosing to withdraw from active participation in solving problems shows that he is unable to cope and has relinquished the power of making decisions to the family. While Herbert knows a great deal on a great variety of subjects, he cannot use his knowledge to construct new ideas by transferring his learning from old situations to new but similar ones. He balks when asked to speculate on possible answers if he does not have a ready made solution which has been given to him by someone else.

This "Withdrawal to Family Dependency" pattern is a manner of coping which relies on an earlier, formerly very secure dependency within the intimate framework of the family. A young child who chooses this pattern of coping has learned not to take the initiative and risk the possible consequences. This makes coping with school problems more difficult since the operative strategy is to accept no new learning unless it has already been transmitted through the family. Since parents are very unlikely to be present during school hours to provide answers, the child has no strategy for coping with new information.

## Rebuilding Confidence by Emphasizing the Child's Personal Best

Herbert is by no means a lost cause. Even though he has emotional problems that are interferring with his potential to learn it is possible to be extremely clear about what these problems are and it is also possible to make specific recommendations about what to do about them (see chapter seven).

However, in order for these recommendations to be effective we must begin to change some of our attitudes about what it means to learn. As well, we will have to change some of our attitudes about how to go about assessing whether learning has occurred.

We have seen from both Herbert and Georgia that it is not enough to simply look at their *performance* in the classroom. One must look deeper, into their *competence*. This is not easy to do and it is for this reason that the model of similarity thinking can be very useful. The development of similarity thinking is essentially the development of the child's competence to bring certain kinds of thinking skills to bear on learning tasks. In our view the child's potential to learn is captured in the way the child uses similarity thinking. A clearer picture of what we mean by learning potential will emerge as we consider the relationship between competence and performance.

When I run ten kilometers I say that I have the ability or competence to run ten kilometers. By the same token when a child learns to add and subtract we say that the child has the ability or competence to add and subtract. When I improve my time to complete a ten kilometer run I say my performance has improved. My *personal best* time to complete the run can be modified by practice. To carry the analogy further, when a child adds and subtracts more quickly, we say the child is demonstrating improved performance because of practice. So clearly the child's performance can be modified through

49

the child's own initiative. Finally, when I take what I have learned running the ten kilometers and apply it to an even longer marathon run, I just might be demonstrating that my competence/performance is at such a high level that I can use it in a new but very similar situation. Likewise, if a child succeeds when given different, but very similar addition and subtraction problems we conclude that the child really does understand (has not simply memorized) and on that basis we may go on to teach a lesson on multiplication.

My personal best may never see me into the Olympics. The child's personal best may never see him or her into the top ten percent of the class. However, in both cases, competence has been demonstrated. Performance has been adequate but it may not have been exceptional. Here is the crux of the matter. When we say a child "has the potential to learn" we must carefully distinguish between one meaning, e.g., that "he or she has the potential to achieve adequate performance" and another meaning, e.g., that "he or she has the potential for exceptional performance." In order to make this kind of distinction we must have some notion of what the theoretical limits of a particular activity might be. In other words we must be able to describe what we mean by exceptional. For example, at one time a four-minute mile was thought to be impossible. However, it was shown that with the proper training the theoretical limits around this performance could be altered, thereby changing what we would accept as being exceptional. Currently there is a great controversy surrounding athletes' use of certain drugs (especially steroids) precisely because the theoretical limits around a variety of athletic events are altered when athletes use these drugs. Like the arms race, everyone is forced to use drugs in order to achieve an equal footing and adequate performance. What is altered as a consequence of this action is the minimum standard or cutting point. Exceptional performance is still possible but the cutting point or merely adequate performance is now described in a different way.

In like manner the child learns what constitutes adequate performance because she is told by the teacher, e.g., "you pass" or "you fail". The child also learns whether his or her performance is exceptional as a consequence of being placed in certain reading and math groups and as a result of teacher comments and grades. The child struggles to achieve equal footing within these groups. Possibly you remember the expression "damned average raiser". Hard working students, like steroids, affect the average result, passing grade or adequate performance cutting point. Consequently it is only the very few children at the "top of their class" who do not feel the constant frustration of seeing adequate performance standards float upwards as a function of their trying harder. For example, the so-called "average child" who tries harder (the damned average-raiser) may be placed in the next "higher" reading group where the adequate performance standard is more difficult. This "average" child, therefore, moves from one group where his performance has undergone improvement (he is exceptional in that group), to another group where this same performance is described as being average. This kind of constant frustration will cause children to perceive themselves as being grossly inadequate. In most cases children stop learning under these conditions. This is exactly where the notion of personal best has most application. Potential to learn is described with reference to where a child has moved. Exceptional performance is described with respect to the degree or amount of changed performance (improvement). When children are praised for this accomplishment as an end in itself and not simply as a means to get into a more difficult group, the cycle of frustration is broken and these children will begin to learn how to learn. They will do this because they will focus on their own personal best and not on some (for them) arbitrary standard. Learning becomes personal and self modifiable. And as children learn how to control their own learning and become more secure in this activity they become more able to engage in the competition of learning: the Olympics of learning. This child begins to set his or her sights on the theoretical limits and those individuals that set the pace.

What exactly are the theoretical limits of "gifted children", the pace-setters? The answer is that these limits are defined by development and that these children are working up to the limits of their development. Adequate performance standards are set by the limits imposed by development. For example, development determines that most children in grade three will only be able to answer questions that ask for the details of what happened in a reading passage. Development determines that by grade six most children will also be able to answer questions that ask for an interpretation of what happened in the reading passage. Therefore, potential to learn is limited by development and personal best cannot go beyond these limits. These ideas are shown in the figure below.

Those children furthest along in development when they are in grade three and when they are in grade six have the potential to be at the top of the class because they have the necessary building blocks (the competence) to accomplish the most. "Average and below average children" will more than likely not be at the same developmental level as the "gifted child". For these children, potential to learn is not of the same order as that for the gifted child in that they do not share the same intellectual building blocks (although for most children

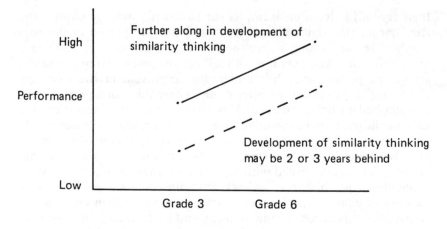

these are in the process of developing). Personal best can be understood with respect to the theoretical limits imposed by development and by the amount of improvement as a result of learning and practice that one can observe from one point in time to another.

We don't know much about Herbert's or Georgia's competence because we don't know how they are developing with respect to similarity thinking. We have the sense that Herbert is not using all of his potential to learn and that Georgia is using a good deal of hers. In any case without knowing how similarity thinking was developing for either Herbert or Georgia, we would have difficulty discussing their potential to learn. The important point to make before we move to the next chapter is that learning is highly individual, influenced as it is by both emotional and developmental factors. The notion of personal best is most useful particularly when we define potential to learn as performance that has been self-modified as an improvement from one point in time to another.

# Chapter 5

# Teachers Can Help Children Organize Their Thinking to Plan Ahead

In the last chapter it was suggested that learning is highly individual and that it is influenced by both emotional and developmental factors. This can leave the teacher somewhat in a quandry as to how to achieve instructional goals.

This chapter will focus on planning skills and the central role of similarity thinking in the acquisition of these skills. We make the claim the the development of planning skills goes hand in hand with children's responsiveness to instruction. Teachers are able to exert considerable influence in the development of planning skills by using particular kinds of instruction and questioning techniques. We show that questioning stimulates children to problem solve as they organize their thinking to respond to these questions. Consequently they begin to attend to information they might otherwise have missed; they take risks they might otherwise have avoided and they develop a mastery over basic skills that they might otherwise not have practiced. In a word, children begin to *anticipate* what they might be asked next and they marshal their resources accordingly. As the teacher responds to individual needs, questions can be tailored to challenge the child's current thinking skills. In this way the child learns how to improve on his or her personal best and simultaneously becomes more independently secure.

## Similarity Thinking, Planning and Instruction

In earlier chapters the point has been made that overview thinking (getting the big picture) makes it possible for children to find a starting place, whether that starting place is selecting a portion of a jigsaw puzzle to work on, beginning to dress starting with a particular article of clothing or working through a math problem starting with a particular operation. In all of these cases children begin to work with

53

things that are familiar and usually where they have experienced some success.

In the last chapter similarity thinking was broken into three clusters where overview thinking was shown to influence both convergent or analytical thought as well as divergent, imagination and creativity. Consequently planning behaviour can occur when overview thinking organizes the perceptual pieces of things like jig-saw puzzles, thereby establishing familiar starting points, as well as when overview thinking organizes divergent ideas to yield novel starting points in problem solving.

The important point about planning behaviour is that children have to consider all of the information at their disposal in order to get an overview. They do this to establish a starting point. They must also do this to get a sense of what the next step might be and more generally to get a sense of the scope of the problem or learning task. Children begin to *anticipate* a direction of activity and thought. They benefit from instruction to the extent that they anticipate correctly so that earlier learning can be used in different but related parts of problems or learning tasks that come later on. In other words children learn to make good or reasonable guesses about what might come later and prepare themselves accordingly.

Teachers can make an important contribution to planning behaviour in the kind of questions that they use to encourage overview thinking. The next section considers questioning techniques in relation to similarity thinking and the stimulation of planning behaviour.

## Questioning Techniques, Similarity Thinking and Planning

Teachers are compelled to meet certain curriculum goals and to evaluate students' mastery of the materials related to achieving these goals. However, teachers are also attempting to respond to the individual needs of their students; trying to help them improve their personal best and in this way helping them achieve the full measure of their potential to learn. Teachers have access to certain teaching skills which are known to have an affect on student learning and which if maximized can help students' achieve organization in their thinking and improvements in planning behaviour. It is important for teachers to realize which aspects of the teaching act and which characteristics of the classroom are within their control and to optimize the learning environment for all students including students with learning problems.

Many of the teacher based influences that affect student performance are rather common sense in nature. When these teaching skills are described most teachers will nod their heads in agreement. For example much has been written on changing the physical arrangement of the classroom, using audio-visual equipment for stimulus variation, changing the teacher's style of interaction by encouraging focusing and gesturing, and by helping the student use different sensory channels. However, these techniques do not allow the teacher to tap directly and efficiently into the students' learning processes.

Perhaps the most engaging, most pervasive and most adaptable teaching skill the classroom teacher can bring to bear in classroom activities is questioning. All teachers recognize the value of questioning techniques as this activity occupies a predominant part of everyday classroom behaviours. However, one of the major drawbacks of questioning as it is frequently used is that it is geared to lesson content rather than to the student's learning process. Furthermore, a student's first answer to a teacher question is often superficial, partial or a guess. Unless the teacher is prepared to probe further into the students thinking, an answer may be dismissed as incorrect and the teacher will move to the next curriculum based question. However, if the teacher uses probing (a systematic questioning technique) the student is required to go beyond a first answer and engage in additional thinking about other possible answers.

The term "probe" is used to mean that the teacher seeks an additional response from the student after a first initial response. Probing is designed to encourage the student to elaborate on or to demonstrate a better understanding than is revealed in this first initial response. Probing techniques are gentle ways to focus students' attention to help them gain an overview of possible answers.

The teacher instead of being tied to a curriculum based lesson plan, proceeds from where the learner actually is. The teacher, according to Orme (1978), must hypothesize about the learner's current level of understanding and must select a probing question which appropriately mediates content goals and the student's response.

The major components of Orme's probing techniques are termed: Refocus, Prompt, Clarify, Critical Awareness, Relation, Predict and Redirect.

Probing techniques encourage students to actively engage in the process of "going beyond the information given". They provide the opportunity for the student to elaborate upon what in many cases is a superficial initial response and to engage in various types of reflective thinking. Students must practice organizing facts and ideas to create a range of possible answers. The answer is expressed as an overt response, an act, which allows the teacher to respond either by reinforcing the answer or by further probing. This way, the teacher assumes the role of decision maker, deciding how to proceed after assessing the student's current level of understanding.

To demonstrate the relationship between probing using systematic questioning strategies and similarity thinking, we describe some research that was conducted by Robertson (1985) with children in grades 3, 4, 5 and 6. The purpose of the research was to explore the relationship between teaching strategies and characteristics of the reflective reasoning process. In other words, Robertson tried by systematically employing higher order probing techniques such as Critical Awareness, Relation and Predict, to get children to shift or to prefer the moral (the more general interpretation) of proverbial sentences. This procedure would directly influence overview thinking aimed as it was at stimulating a more general overview.

A rather innovative methodology was used to test the assumption that the use of higher order questioning would facilitate children's comprehension of figurative language. A proverb task was used, for example:

*You cannot eat your cake and keep it too*
1. You can either eat your cake or keep it (CL)
2. Sometimes you can do only one of two things (CA)
3. Sometimes you can do everything that you want to do
4. You can eat your cake and ask for more

The response alternatives yield measures of children's understanding of (a) a correct literal interpretation of the proverb, (b) a correct and more abstract meaning of the proverb, in other words, the moral of the proverb and (c) an indication of which meaning the children preferred. They were asked to check off two sentences that had about the same meaning as the proverb and then indicate which of the two checked sentences was the better meaning. Looking at the results of the pretest from a developmental perspective, we see that the youngest children chose the literal alternative. Children slightly older were more likely to choose the moral since they are beginning to develop advanced overview thinking skills. However, only children in the oldest age bracket consistently prefered the moral of the proverb.

Having these pretest results, Robertson wanted to see whether she could get children to change their orientation to the proverbs as a result of being exposed to different questioning techniques. She expected that when children viewed a videotaped microteaching session of a lesson on proverbs where the predominant questioning technique used by the teacher was higher order probing, that they would choose and prefer the moral of the proverb over the more literal meaning alternatives. Conversely, she expected that when children viewed a comparable microteaching session where the predominant questioning technique was lower order probing that children would prefer the literal meaning alternative. In both conditions children had additional opportunity for "hands-on" practice when the teacher continued the questioning strategies being demonstrated on tape using semi-programmed scripts. These follow-up teacher question student response interactions were appropriately matched to the videotapes that had preceeded them. The scripts for the videotapes of the micro-teaching sessions are included in the appendix.

The results of the study clearly demonstrated that children significantly change their preferences towards the moral of the proverb when they are exposed to questioning techniques which direct and probe their reflective thinking. Conversely, children, especially older children, changed their preference from the moral of the proverb to a more literal alternative when the probes they were exposed to only required clarification or reiteration.

The implication of these kinds of results is that the teacher has considerable influence in terms of the quality of response that can be elicited from students. When teachers are skilled in their questioning techniques, students will have the opportunity to clarify issues, examine more possibilities for materials, attend to relevant information and self-question or reflect on their own thinking. These are all of the necessary strategies that children must use to make the best use of their problem solving abilities.

The results for the proverb task in this research are of particular importance for relating questioning techniques to similarity thinking. In order to more completely understand a proverb, children must move away from the specific or the literal meaning of the statement to a more general meaning or the moral which applies to more life situations than the one illustrated by the proverb. They must in a sense come up with an overview meaning which would include many different but possible occasions when the proverb (moral) would be appropriate. Probing techniques gently push children beyond a literal interpretation to consider these possible applications. As children reflect on their reasoning, they come to see that the most general meaning is the better meaning simply because there are more possiblities for the application of the moral. The teacher is then in an ideal position to encourage students to *anticipate* when a proverb might be used and in this way stimulate students to plan ahead using overview thinking.

# When Things Go Wrong in Planning

Under optimal conditions most children respond to questions that organize their thinking to plan ahead. On the other hand there are some children who do not respond and who consequently do not develop overview thinking. This problem has been described by Kinsbourne and Caplan (1979) as follows:

> Some children fail because they are overly impulsive and do not maintain their focus of attention long enough to learn the material. Although their thinking equipment is adequate, they leave a task before the concept involved is fully grasped. They have the necessary processing potential for grade-school readiness, but they are immature with respect to the intensity and duration of their concentration as well as their ability to maintain a focus of attention on the task at hand. (p. 3)

There is some controversy as to what is the cause of "impulsive" behaviour. Ross (1976) suggests that children begin to act impulsively if they are confronted too often with questions that are too difficult for them to solve. They soon find that difficult problems cause a lot of anxiety and the quickest way to reduce that anxiety it is to get the unpleasantness over as soon as possible. "Better to give the wrong answer quickly than to struggle for a long time only to find that the answer is wrong anyway." A more physically active youngster may accomplish the same end by turning from one task to another leaving a long list of unfinished projects. This child literally escapes from one failed task to the next hoping that he or she might have a better chance of succeeding in a new task whereas failure is a certainty in the present one. Ross suggests that this impulsive movement "might well be the behaviour which earns such children the labels hyperactive and distractible" (p. 121).

An important piece of research into impulsive strategies was carried out by Egeland (1974) with a group of seventy-two impulsive children. His experiment showed very strong evidence that impulsivity can be changed. He trained the children with rules designed to persuade them to adopt the following procedures:

> Attend to the relevant details ... to examine alternatives, to break down the alternatives into their components parts, to look for similarities and differences, and to eliminate alternatives until only the correct alternative remained.

Egeland concluded that the impulsive thinking style used by many children is not so much the cause of their academic problems, but the effect that failure has had on their approach to problem solving. It appears that impulsive responding is a method that children learn as a result of their failing at problem solving.

Similarly, Johnson (1979) has demonstrated that impulsive children can be taught to pay attention to the relevant aspects of a problem. He found that a six-year old who had been diagnosed as having an impulsive style made 15 errors on an auditory discrimination test which matched sounds to pictures. When the test was repeated with the examiner holding the child's hand and encouraging him to look at all the pictures carefully before responding, the child made only one error. The same child was given a picture vocabulary test and scored at the 4-year level when no precautions were taken to prevent impulsive behaviour. He scored at the 6-year-old level when controls for impulsivity were used. Johnson cautions teachers to beware of using group administered reading tests because many impulsive children make choices without attending to all the questions and possible alternatives.

We take the view that impulsivity is a *state* not a *trait*. We believe that learning strategies are modifiable. The questioning techniques described in the last section provide concrete suggestions for stimulating children to modify their learning strategies. We find that there are a significant number of children in every classroom who could benefit from this kind of instruction.

The following case study described by Russ Fleming is a fairly typical example of a child who has not learned how to organize her thinking to plan ahead.

## Josie

At one point I taught a little girl, Josie, who seemed to have some difficulty in learning. The problem was an unusual one because she was able to do so many of the things that the other children could do when supervised, but left to work on her own, her work was unsatisfactory. After observing her for a period of time, it seemed apparent that lack of organization was the basis of her problem.

Attending Josie's high school graduation was a truly satisfying experience for me. When I entered the auditorium I could see Josie's famous smile radiating right to the very back of the auditorium. She was impeccably dressed, being one of the few people I have known who possess a perfect sense of colour and fashion.

While organization in her academic subjects frequently caused her problems, her artistic talents were always apparent. I remember that as a young child of ten she had mastered certain skills in art. She could take the most ordinary or materials and transform them into works of startling beauty. Teachers would often ask to keep her creations to brighten their days.

When meeting Josie she projected a sense of warmth and confidence which belied the truth of her daily experiences in school. In her academic work she was often confused. I vividly recall how she would come to me for help with instructions that other children found very straightforward and easy to carry out.

There was an experience with a drum which I shall never forget. We were studying "Canada's Native People" and had settled on a project. The project was to include a trip to the museum where the children would examine the Indian artifacts. Each child carried some drawing material so that they could make sketches from the display cases. The sketches were to be used as a sort of blueprint for the manufacture of artifacts back at the school.

The museum outing was very successful and we arrived back in the classroom with many drawings to examine. The next day we conducted a sorting session where we examined the diagrams and selected the ones most suitable for the materials we had at hand. As usual, Josie's drawings were outstanding, she had even remembered the colours which she quickly added with her own pastels.

Some of the children continued to ponder their drawings for a time before choosing materials for the project. Josie was not indecisive; she had been immediately excited by the sight of an Indian drum and had decided to reproduce it when she arrived back in the classroom. She sat to work selecting the materials she would use for the project. In spite of her initial decisiveness about selecting a project, I noticed that she spent an inordinately long time in the materials box. In fact, by the time she made her choice the other children had already selected their materials and had been at work for some period of time.

When she had finally chosen the materials she arrived at my desk, beaming as usual, with a single board and a coping saw. I was quite perplexed by her choice of materials and enquired how she intended to use such rigid materials to make an instrument which is as flexible as a drum. The explanation that followed was quite baffling to me, but Josie seemed confident that she had made the right selection and so I found her some space on a work bench so that she could proceed. I could not imagine however, just how the drum she had drafted so magnificently on paper would ever emerge from that board.

Each day we worked on the project. Josie would bring out her materials and work with great gusto and satisfaction. However, at the end of each day's work I was no closer to understanding the construction of the drum that I was the day before. Since I thoroughly believe in letting children work through their problems to make their own discoveries, I found that I had suppress the urge to tell her how to proceed to make the drum.

I found myself frequently drawn to where she was working. I attempted to make myself helpful by showing her how to use the vice, or make a saw stroke. In the process of helping, I always enquired about the project. Her reaction was always the same – she was marvellous and her project was doing very nicely, thank you very much.

I remember that her "revelation" came at the end of the third day. I remember looking up and seeing her changed expression from across the room. Her usual radiant smile had been replaced by a look of total disbelief. I watched for a moment and then walked over to where she was working. Kneeling down beside her, so that we were both at the same eye level, I asked her what was wrong. When she eventually heard me, she turned her head slowly and replied in an astonished voice, "... I can't play it ... can I?"

It is hard to imagine why Josie could not see from the outset that her drum was not at all like the wonderful drum that she had so diligently drawn in the museum. Certainly, the other children who were working nearby on their own projects had appeared as perplexed about the "drum" as I had felt. For some reason Josie was so compelled by some aspects of the drum she could not attend to all of its aspects. Perhaps the colours and shape attracted her. In any case it took her a long time to ask herself whether it would actually work to make a drum sound.

## Organizing Thinking to Plan Ahead

Many researchers including those cited above have commented on cases like Josie's. For example, Douglas (1972; 1974a) found that:

> These youngsters are apparently unable to ... cope with situations in which care, concentrated attention, or organized planning are required. They tend to react ... to those aspects of a situation which are the most obvious or compelling ... The fundamental cause of their maladaptive behaviour lies in their ability to focus, sustain and organize attention ... (In Ross, 1976, p. 109).

There seemed to be two sides to Josie, one with a well developed talent for colour and design and the other, an individual whose performance was less than satisfactory when trying to initiate and organize projects which required her to understand the consequences of her actions. Symptomatic of her problem was the fact that she became noticeably confused, as indicated by her characteristic blank stare when asked to carry out a number of things in succession such as putting away her pencil, placing her book on the shelf and lining up for dismissal.

Unlike many children experiencing academic difficulties, Josie could read many of the passages in her reader once she became familiar with them. Much of her spelling was quite acceptable for her age and grade level. On the other hand, she seemed to have trouble deriving meaning from unfamiliar passages in her reader unless the questions were factual in nature. She also had problems following events in a sequence, for instance, if she was asked to follow along in a story and read a passage when her turn came, she invariably could not find the place where the last child was reading. In math, she often lost her place when trying to add a column of numbers.

Josie's level of intellectual ability did not seem to account for her academic problems. In fact, the results of intelligence testing showed that she scored quite within the normal range for children her age. The only clue about the difficulties she experienced in school work was that she seemed to need to hide herself away in a quiet corner of the room when she wanted to concentrate on some unfamiliar problem.

## A Developmental View of Overview Thinking and Planning

Organizing thinking to plan ahead begins early in development and as in Josie's case it is difficult to remediate this kind of deficiency later on. In an earlier chapter we showed that overview thinking and planning behaviour begins when the child uses the pronoun "I" because a knowledge of "self" provides a reference point for planning. Between the ages of three and six children begin exchanging "me" and "mine" for "I" as they begin to take their own initiatives. The pronoun "I" is much more useful than "me" or "mine" as the need grows to talk about themselves doing things and playing cooperatively with others.

Another aspect of "self" which is a necessary part of organizing for planning is the knowledge of one's own body. One indicator of a child's growing knowledge of his or her own body is the ability to draw a person. According to Shirley Vulpé, when young children from two and a half to three years of age draw a picture of a person, they include only the "head and body or head with eyes, nose and mouth". However, by the time children are four and a half to five years of age they are drawing "a figure with head and body, arms, legs, feet, mouth, nose and eyes" (1969, pp. 204-5). As the knowledge of one's body becomes organized, so does the knowledge of other objects which surround oneself.

David, the boy in chapter two who was able to use the pronoun "I", used language to plan his role in helping his mother. He could communicate his intentions by saying, "I am putting the knives on the table." As indicated previously, he has already become interested in cooperative play and he spends a great deal of time watching other children play. When he begins to play cooperatively he will use the pronoun "I" since he will need words which can separate his own initiatives from those of the other children. Later, the development of his language and overview thinking skills will allow him to look ahead and plan more elaborate projects.

Nursery and kindergarten teachers have long been aware of the importance of teaching common prepositions. One of the most significant uses of the preposition by young children is the advantage that it provides for planning. A preposition such as "beside" serves as a means of positioning an object in relationship to the person who is doing the planning. Initially, children learn a preposition like "beside" as a place name, as in the phrase "the doll beside the box". Later on, children will learn that "beside" is a relative term. If they are standing in a different position in relation to the box the doll may be "behind" the box.

Prepositions such as "beside", "behind" and "in front of" are often first understood as a place name when children are two years and a half to three years of age. Later on, each of these prepositions can be used by children to communicate the relative positions of objects. Still later, children learn to understand the position of an object by putting themselves in another child's shoes. When two children are sitting across the table from each other and one says that the salt is "behind" the butter, it is clear from the other child's point of view that it is "in front of" the butter. The second child will understand the sentence in a very complete way when the first child's point of view is understood. Advances in the ability to plan ahead depend upon children not only acquiring a perspective of their own but the perspective of others as well. This is another way of describing what happens when children get the big picture or achieve an overview.

In early childhood there are many occasions when parents and teachers use language that implies that activities should proceed in a particular sequence. In order to understand the "why" of the sequence it is necessary to have an overview of the entire task. For example when children are first learning to dress themselves, they may not have an overview. Consequently, they find themselves trying to pull on their trousers over their shoes or trying to do up a zipper after they have put on their mittens. However by 4–5 years of age children have begun to develop more complete overview thinking skills which enable them to understand concepts like "first", "second", and "last". This allows them to choose the appropriate object when a series of objects are placed in a line. Once children have learned that words like first, second and last can order objects in relation to one another they are able to follow instructions on practical tasks such as getting dressed.

When children have learned to look ahead systematically using language like "first", "second", and "last", they need practice monitoring various learning tasks. They should be taught to periodically check on their own progress whenever they are performing a task. Teachers and parents can help children monitor their own progress by asking them, "What comes next?" or enquire as to "what" they are buiding. Even young children can monitor their own behaviour when adults help them. For instance, a kindergarten teacher who stops to help a child assemble a puzzle may say, "What are you going to do when you finish the puzzle? Remember that the pieces go in the box and then you put them away on the shelf."

## The Emotional Consequence of Having Inadequate Planning Skills

Children who have not sufficiently practiced overview thinking are not able to adequately plan ahead. Because these children often begin tasks without adequate preparation there is a constant need for them to check on the progress of others instead of relying on their own personal skills. These children may seem to continually nag to find out what to do next so that teachers may find themselves saying, "Why can't you do that for yourself? None of the other children have to ask me how to do every little thing."

The annoyance that both teachers and parents feel in this kind of situation is often due to the overly dependent nature of these children since they must continually refer to the adult in order to progress with a task. However, with the refusal of adults to cooperate these children often resort to excuses, rationalizing their inability to plan a task by saying such things as, "I don't know how."

In fact these children usually are quite capable of carrying out various tasks but only when they receive help organizing the materials and only when someone else makes the decision about where to start. This dependency on others as "adopted agents" will often interfere with these children becoming independently secure. We have noted this pattern developing for Herbert in chapter four and will see more symptoms in Richard's behaviour described in the next chapter. We offer specific suggestions for remediating this problem in chapter seven. For now we simply suggest that many children have had inadequate opportunities to practice overview thinking so as to develop strong planning skills. We point out that there is a consequence for the emotional development of these children.

## Summary

In this chapter we have shown that overview thinking is modifiable. Children even early on in development can be given direction to help them organize their thinking and encouragement to plan ahead. Similarity thinking is instrumental in achieving this objective. When children are able to benefit from instruction and plan ahead they are beginning to transfer old learning to new situations. This ability to generalize is fundamental to being able to adapt to new life situations and in this sense it is directly related to the emotional life of the child. In the next chapter we describe a dynamic assessment of similarity thinking and in subsequent chapters we return to the consequence of this way of thinking for the emotional development of the child.

Chapter 6

# The Assessment of Similarity Thinking: A Case Study

We present a case study in this chapter using the assessment of similarity thinking to make some important points about learning potential. We want to stress that in our view learning potential is modifiable. This is why it is possible to give children hints or clues about what the assessment tasks are asking them to do, *during the assessment itself.* You cannot help children too much in this kind of assessment. Indeed, we want to determine whether children can benefit from instruction in terms of the *amount* of help they require and in terms of the *kind* of help that seems to make a difference to their understanding and subsequently to their performance on the assessment tasks. Although we want to know what children bring to the assessment situation, we are particularly interested in their *responsiveness* to the kinds of aid we provide to help them understand what these tasks are asking them to do. One kind of evidence for learning potential is therefore reflected in the child's ability to profit from instruction. Another kind of evidence for learning potential can be found in children's ability to generalize or tranfer old information to different but related situations. This is one reason why similarity thinking is so important; it helps children notice what is familiar or similar in new situations. Similarity thinking therefore helps children generalize from the old to the new. In this book we do not give examples of tasks that assess for children's ability to generalize, nor do we provide examples of the graduated aids we use to help children understand the nature of the assessment tasks. This kind of detailed analysis belongs in the next book in the series on Learning Potential. Here, we want to share our attitude about the importance of assessing for the potential to learn as opposed to assessing for what the child can already achieve. We also want to describe what we mean by similarity thinking by showing you some of the tasks we use in the assessment. Children have individual needs by the very fact that they may be in different places with respect to similarity thinking. It is almost impossible to talk about "normative" behaviour because children can be two to three years apart in the development of similarity thinking even though they may share the same chronological age.

The importance of similarity thinking for emotional development can be found in the next chapter, Therapy for the Sane Child. Some of the difficulties teachers encounter attempting to respond to individual needs can be found in the chapter following our discussion of emotional development.

# Introducing Richard

Peter couldn't understand what had gone wrong for his son at school. Richard was seven and a half, mid-way through grade 2, and without prior warning the school was saying that he had problems learning. Peter felt that the school had simply "dumped" these problems on him and his wife, and he couldn't understand why nothing had been done when Richard was in grade 1.

When Peter went to the school to get some answers he discovered that it was school policy not to put much pressure on children at the grade one level, counting on the child to mature, to grow into being able to meet the school's expectations for work habits by grade 2. For whatever reasons this had not happened for Richard. Consequently, from Peter's point of view Richard had missed out on one and one-half years of basic skills.

From the school's perspective Richard's basic skills were not up to par mainly because of behaviour problems: lack of motivation and responsibility for starting and completing work; not listening, and generally causing a disruption in the classroom. Peter's response was that he knew his own kid pretty well and that from his "gut level" he felt that Richard was bright and had the potential to learn. He gave examples of Richard's behaviour at home doing things like providing elaborations on sophisticated concepts. These examples contrasted with what happened at school were it was the teacher's view that Richard could not elaborate and did not have a sophisticated vocabulary. Peter's response to this was an angry one, asserting that there must be something going on at school that was somehow lowering Richard's self-concept and self-esteem, consequently interferring with his ability to demonstrate what he was capable of doing at home.

Peter was more than ready to admit that his son at times "marched to a different drummer". Since Peter was the coach of a local soccer team and actually "coached" his own son, he was able to provide some insight into Richard's behaviour at school. From Peter's point of view there had been three kinds of kids on his teams over the years. One third of these children needed no help at all other than various kinds of encouragement. One third occasionally needed pointers and extra practice around basic skills. One third needed constant supervision, had difficulty staying on task and more generally were not there to play soccer. Richard belonged to the last third in Peter's estimation. Richard would act the clown on the field, distracting the other players, requiring quite a lot of supervision and discipline to keep him on track. Peter responded to his behaviour by providing more rules and structure and most importantly immediate consequences for Richard's behaviour. Peter noticed that it wasn't that Richard did not have the basic skills to play soccer because once he understood the consequences of his "clown" behaviour (that it was unacceptable) he began to demonstrate his real potential. In a word, Peter felt that the school and teacher should be "on" Richard to work in the classroom. Peter felt that his approach on the soccer field could be used in the classroom.

As a result of Peter's discussions with the teacher and principal a school psychologist began observing Richard in the clasroom. Subsequent discussion with the psychologist left Peter with the impression that the school system staff had given up on Richard, that he was a "hopeless case" and would never amount to anything. Whether Peter was accurate in these impressions is really not the issue. This was the interpretation that this particular parent came away with. Peter was concerned that Richard's record would be tarnished and conceivably that he might be placed in a class for slow learners. Consequently, Peter sought outside help either to confirm or disconfirm his impression that Richard had the potential to learn. He made an appointment to meet the Director of the Learning Skills Development Centre.

## The Assessment of Similarity Thinking

All clients at the Centre are referred to specialists for independent assessment of possible hearing and/or visual motor impairment. Quite simply, many "learning problems" can be traced to difficulties in these areas. Subsequently it was learned that Richard had no problems with hearing. However, his visual memory and visual motor skills were another matter.

Richard had two kinds of visual problems: He triple focused; instead of one letter he would see three letters blurred together. And he also had difficulties with visual memory; remembering what a design looked like after it had been presented for only a few seconds. When it came to copying the design, Richard produced something that looked completely different. Just imagine trying to remember and copy a design when you have a triple focusing problem. Imagine what it must have been like for Richard to print and read letters at school.

The specialist had seen many children like Richard. He felt that Richard's visual perceptual skills were very immature. In his view with exercises and maturation these skills would improve dramatically. He felt that Richard was a bright boy with potential who would excel in the future. Furthermore he felt that Richard's visual deficiencies were highly related to the kinds of attentional problems he was told Richard was demonstrating at school. In his experience, children like Richard get "locked into themselves" possibly because they have some sense that there is a problem. Consequently, again in the specialist's view, Richard would not (at least in the near future) be able to do a speed drill where reading or copying was a prerequisite. One would get one set of results on a standardized test where time is controlled and a different set of results when Richard could proceed at his own pace.

The most appropriate kind of assessment for Richard is one where he is not timed. Instead we want to determine how he goes about the task; what sorts of decisions he makes; the types of strategies he uses; how far he gets in the problem solving process; whether he is ultimately successful. We also want to understand how much attention Richard can bring to bear on the tasks; whether he is able to take risks; what kind of supportive environment he requires to sustain his attention and finally how tolerant he is of his own behaviour. For example, does he applaud his attempts and continue on with the task?

## Thinking I Tasks

Richard was given Thinking I tasks like the one on page 71. He was asked to look at the cat on the left and to indicate which one of the others on the right was most like it. After he pointed to one of the four cats it was covered with a piece of cardboard and he was asked which one of the remaining three cats was most like the cat on the left. Of course the adult always helped Richard understand what the target was and what the alternatives were. After Richard's second choice was covered he was asked which of the remaining two cats was most like the one on the left.

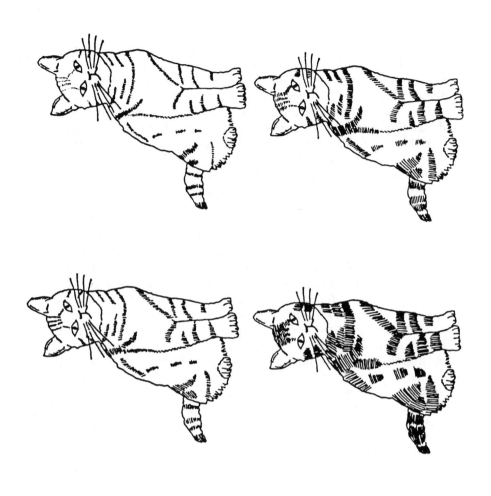

Fig. 1
Cat task

71

Using this procedure we determine whether Richard can construct a "most like" continuum using the cat on the left as a reference point. We determine whether Richard understands relative similarity which means that he understands that one thing is most like another depending upon the context of alternatives. He might say "this one over here (on the right) is most like this one (on the left) but only when I can't see this one" (because it had been covered). Using these procedures we determine how flexible Richard is with respect to comparing objects in the context of other objects when he must keep in mind a target goal (the cat on the left). In this example you can see how relative similarity thinking is a kind of part-whole thinking – the whole includes the target and alternatives (the whole set). Richard must compare a subset of parts to each other (the four alternatives) and each one of these alternatives to the target – and so on as each one of his choices is covered. The key word here is *flexibility*.

In order to be flexible Richard must understand that his "most like" answer always depends on the context. As a result the "correct" answer changes in the context. Notice that Thinking I depends upon information coming into the perceptual system. All of the criterial information can be observed. Subsequently Richard must use relative similarity mental operations to organize what he observes into a "most like" continuum. Another way of describing this perceptual information is to say that it is holistic. Richard must determine that there is a "most like" order based on the intensity or darkness of the target and alternatives. There is nothing to count in Type I tasks.

Richard's triple focusing and visual memory problems presented no difficulty for him in this or in any of the Thinking I tasks. He thought the tasks "terrifically humorous" and had no problem understanding what the tasks were asking him to do. We conclude that Richard has considerable flexibility in making similarity judgements for Thinking I tasks.


## Thinking II Tasks

Richard was given Thinking II tasks like the one on page 73. These tasks are very similar to Thinking I tasks except that the child is asked to point to an alternative that is identical to the target even though the same instruction "most like" is used. This requires greater precision and accuracy than was the case for the Thinking I tasks. Greater accuracy is possible because there are discrete features that can be counted. When children understand that counting is an appropriate strategy to use in Thinking II tasks, they will use that strategy (Gam-

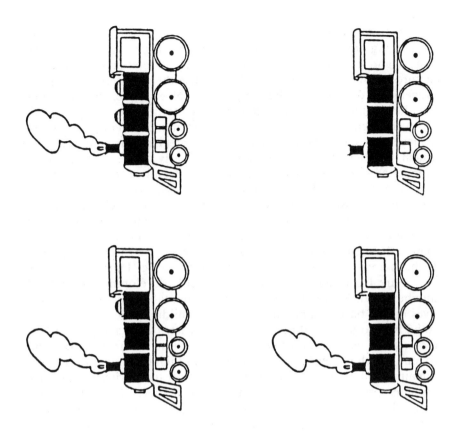

Fig. 2
Train task

lin, 1982; Allan, 1984; Rizwan, 1984). This is a conceptual strategy for judging amount in that a unique number tag is assigned to each feature and a cardinal value is assigned to the total amount of these features. However children continue to use their perception to make judgements of amount. They might say, for example, that it "looks like there is more in this one than in these" (other alternatives). Obviously children who rely on perceptual information exclusively cannot achieve the same level of accuracy or precision as children who attach numbers to their perceptions. Clearly, these "systems" for judging amount are not mutually exclusive. Notice that Thinking II tasks are virtually identical to Thinking I tasks once children have selected as "most like" the alternative that exactly matches the target. Therefore, unless the difference between the numbers of features in each alternative is very close, children can rely on the more approximate judgements of amount provided by their "holistic" perceptions. Perhaps now it is somewhat clearer how Thinking II similarity judgements are more dependent upon children's developing concepts of number. In tasks which require fine discriminations between alternatives on the basis of amount of features, children who do not understand how to use counting will be at a greater disadvantage. Furthermore, when children must select between these alternatives to identify one which is identical to the target and then continue to order the remaining alternatives according to the "most like" criterion, the task becomes prohibitive. On the other hand, if there is a greater "distance" between the amount of features in each alternative (the number of features in each alternative is very different) then children can rely exclusively upon their perceptual system for making relative most like similarity judgements.

It would seem that children who have counting or number concepts have more potential for *flexibility* in that they are able to shift between conceptual (number) and perceptual "systems" as a function of the demands of the task. Richard demonstrated that he has this kind of flexibility. He used a counting strategy when it was appropriate to do so. Once again in spite of his triple focusing problem, he was able to equivalence match and correctly order alternatives along the "most like" continuum.

## Thinking III Tasks

An example of a Thinking III task is on page 76. In this task the object is to make the path longer by using up all of the alternatives on the right. Notice that two of the alternatives could fit right after the first three joined together in the target. However only one of these alternatives makes it possible to join up the rest. In a Thinking III task it is necessary to consider all the possibilities for the whole set of target and pathway pieces in order to achieve the goal (use up all the pieces in one continuous pathway). When children are successful on a Thinking III task they are demonstrating an understanding of means-end relationships. The last piece is *similar* to the first piece in that both pieces are joined together by other pieces on the basis of the same rule thereby making it possible to achieve the goal. As for Thinking II tasks, children may use conceptual (number) and/or perceptual "systems" to join the pieces together.

Possibly because Richard had a perceptual problem, he was not content simply to match the ends of the pathways while taking acount of how the remaining pieces would fit together. He counted the number of spaces up to the join between each pair of alternatives. He was also flexible, in that he was able to revise his orderings of pieces once he realized he could not use up all of them in one continuous pathway. We can say then that Richard had a firm grasp of means-end relationships when all of the information was present and amenable to perceptual organization. He was able to correctly sequence the alternative pieces even when (as for some of the Thinking III tasks) he had to make connections across gaps of space (where there was no visible means to join the pieces. He was also able to "check" his performance by using a conceptual (number) strategy.

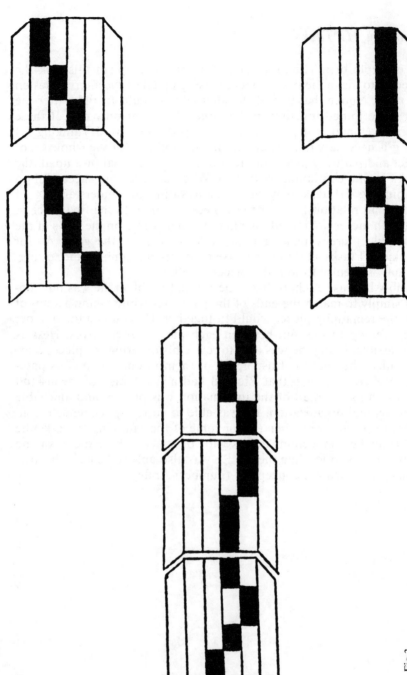

Fig.3
Pathway task

## Thinking IV Tasks

Richard was given Thinking IV tasks like this:

---

### Hockey-stick: PUCK
### Baseball-bat:  ?

---

Fig. 4
Analogy task

Thinking IV tasks investigate how flexible the child is with respect to using conceptual rules to put things together. In this analogy problem, the method (of analogizing) determines how one comparison pair (Hockey-stick: Puck) "sets up" the other (Baseball-bat: ?). The relationship of Hockey-stick and Puck is "carried over" to Baseball-bat and ?. The child is helped by the method of analogy to draw an *inference* about what would go with Baseball-bat using the example of Puck going with Hockey-stick. These analogies using Type IV thinking do not require a "great conceptual leap" in inferencing since the pairings are closely associated and usually familiar. Indeed many six to eight-years olds (and some five-year olds) routinely succeed on these tasks.

Richard had no difficulty with these kinds of tasks. He used the method of analogy to decide that hockey-sticks and baseball-bats are similar, not only because thay are used in sports activities but also because of the analogy itself, e.g., pucks "go with" hockey sticks *in a similar way* as baseballs "go with" baseball-bats.

Thinking IV requires children to go beyond using their perceptions as an exclusive basis for comparing things. In both Thinking III joining tasks and Thinking IV analogy tasks children increasingly come to think about what they are doing and where it is all leading. Plans are more deliberate as children begin to act intentionaly in order to achieve some goal. Children begin to revise plans on the basis of means-end considerations. This kind of mental activity means that children are beginning to understand their experience not only directly through perception but also indirectly by increasingly using symbols to "stand-for" direct perceptual experience. When symbols are substituted for the direct perception of things it is possible to ask "what-if" questions mainly because symbols can be manipulated. For example, Thinking IV makes it possible to ask "what if" hockey-sticks and baseball-bats were compared? What would you learn *if* you compared them? The method of analogy facilitates this comparison since it "pulls out" one basis for the comparison (the relationship of hockey-stick to puck).

"What-if" questions foreshadow hypothesis-making and hypothesis-testing. Both require the use of symbols and symbols manipulation. It is in this sense that Thinking IV makes it possible to derive insight from earlier experience (to reinterpret earlier experience), since the application of rules to symbols leads to new discoveries.

Richard was given two additional kinds of Thinking IV tasks to determine to what extent his ability to use rules had progressed.

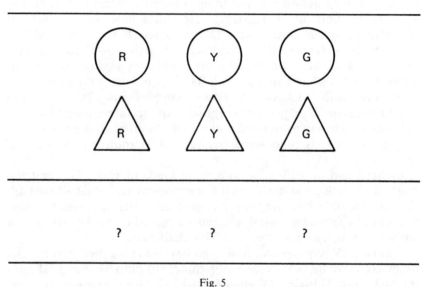

Fig. 5
Colour sequence task

Red, yellow and green plastic geometric figures were arranged as shown above: He was given an assortment of nine additional figures where only the squares repeated the colours red, yellow, and green. Richard was able to use the colour sequence rule to select and appropriately place the squares. This means that he was able to separate colour from form in order to focus on the rule.

Richard was also given the following task:

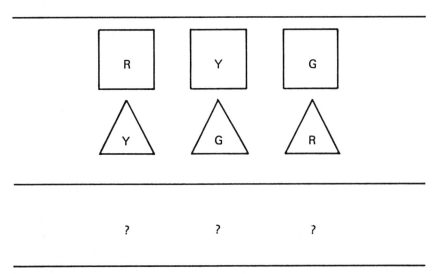

Fig. 6
Permutation task

He was supplied with a variety of plastic shapes that were comprised of six different colours. In order to successfully complete this task Richard had to separate colour from form, and in addition he had to use a "permutation" rule. He had to notice that the second line of figures began with the second colour in the first row. The permutation rule would allow Richard to select any figure as long as it was green and place it at the beginning of the third row. He would however have to check to see that this figure was available in red and yellow. If it was, then he would put the red one next and the yellow last. This is exactly what Richard was able to do.

From these and other Thinking IV results we conclude that Richard is able to perform some very sophisticated symbol manipulations. He is gaining proficiency in asking "what if" questions and he is able to plan ahead in order to anticipate what he will need next in order to achieve his goals.

"What if" questions come directly out of similarity thinking right across Thinking III through VII. The child develops increasing flexibility in proposing "what if" comparisons between ideas, objects and events that on the surface might look like they cannot possibly be compared. Making discoveries about how things go together often leads to new solutions for old problems. Although we do not compare Piaget's theory of intellectual development to similarity thinking in this book, for those familiar with Piaget's theory, we describe Richard as being in transition, no longer exclusively concrete operational, but moving toward using formal operational rules in his thinking.

### Thinking V Skills

Thinking V is holistic, "big picture" and overview oriented, somewhat fashionably called "right-brain" directed. This is contrasted with Thinking IV which could be described as "left-brain" directed. In the similarities theory both Thinking IV and V mature in the same timeframe between five and seven years. The major contribution of Thinking V is precisely its holistic properties. Thinking V does not get bogged-down in the subroutines of mental operations. For example, the child using the picture supplied with a jig-saw-puzzle does not stop when two pieces do not go-together. Rather, the child refers back to the picture as a whole, makes another decision about where to begin and continues on. Perhaps you can understand how thinking V complements Thinking III and IV. Thinking V supports and builds on the planning aspects of thinking IV and Thinking III. Goal attainment is more probable when you have "the big picture" because coming up with the means to achieve these goals is more easily accomplished. One idea that is only mentioned here but will be pursued in Thinking VI is that Thinking V often helps to produce *flexibility* with respect to the means used to achieve goals. Having a goal clearly in mind makes it possible to consider a "better" solution, perhaps with respect to existing resources, time, cost and so on.

Richard was given a picture-problem like that on page 81. When "background", big-picture information is used in this problem, it is possible to decide where each of the four circles "fit". This picture-problem is not unlike a jig-saw puzzle where "background" information also helps you select the next piece.

Sometimes, however, in order to get the big-picture it is necessary to disregard the background and focus instead on the "foreground". To find out whether Richard could do this he was given a a picture-problem like that on page 82. He was asked whether he could find a familiar object hidden in the picture. Whenever he could not, he was given the geometric pieces that comprised the hidden figure, but not joined into any recognizable form. He was asked to use these pieces to find the hidden picture. In order to succeed, Richard would have to use "foreground" information while he tried to ignore the background pieces that camouflaged the hidden figure.

80

Fig. 7
Background design task

81

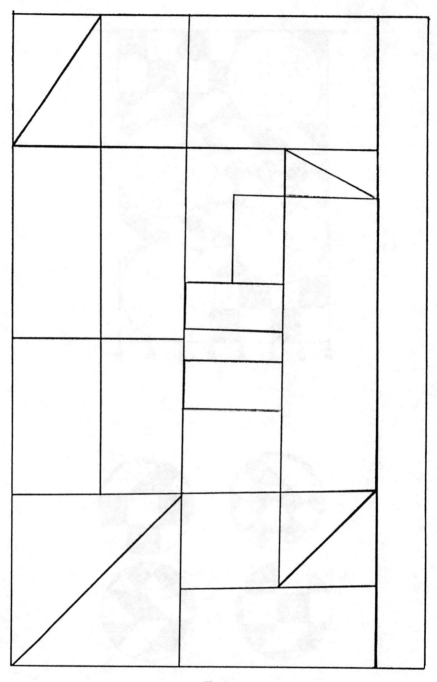

Fig. 8
Camouflaged ship task

Richard had no difficulty using both foreground and background information to get the "big-picture", although for some picture-problems he did require the extra help of seeing the geometric pieces making up the hidden figure separate from the picture-problem as a whole. Once again Richard's perceptual problems did not interfere with his performance on these tasks.

Foregrounding and backgrounding holistic thinking V skills are often used conjointly to get the big-picture, something like using a zoom lens, focusing "wide-angle" to get as much background as possible at one point in time and then "zooming-in" to get close up and detail on another occasion.

Getting the big-picture often involves trying out both foregrounding and backgrounding operations. One of the best tasks for assessing this kind of flexibility was designed by Grace Arthur (1944). The Stencil Design Test looks something like this:

Fig. 9
Stencil design task

The child is given a "picture" card comprised of geometric forms and colours. The child's task is to overlap different "parts" to achieve "the big picture". The child must overlap the separate cards in the correct sequence in order to construct an identical design to the one on the "picture" card. The "picture" cards in the Stencil Design Test vary in difficulty such that the simplest design requires overlapping two cards while the most difficult requires overlapping seven. We stress that the terminology used here is unique to this book and not to the Stencil Design Test since it is our sole intention to point to the usefulness of this kind of material for assessing Thinking V. Notice that this task requires "zooming-out" to see the picture-card as a whole and "zooming-in" to compare pairs, triples or some sub-set of cards in the effort of "building-up" to the design as a whole.

Richard was able to overlap four separate cards in the correct sequence to make a design identical to the one on the "picture" card. He was able to do this for several "picture" cards. According to the norms established for the Stencil Design Test this is what one would expect for an individual Richard's age. For our purpose it is significant how well Thinking III, IV and V complement one another in Richard's case. Clearly Richard is able to use sequence information and engage in symbol manipulation in a quite sophisticated fashion. There is no question that he uses Thinking V "big picture" expertise as he goes about applying Thinking III and IV. Interestingly his triple focusing and visual memory problems seem not to interfere in these kinds of tasks.

## Thinking VI Tasks

Thinking VI, in a word, is the ability to be innovative. This means that children must use the rule systems of Thinking IV and the overview, "big picture" skills of Thinking V, in *different* ways than they have in the past. We can understand Thinking VI with reference to games like chess where the rules are known beforehand and the object of the game is clearly stated. Being innovative in chess is to use the old rules at the service of new patterns. Pattern-making in chess requires anticipating the consequence of moving a piece or pieces some moves later as well as anticipating the opponent's moves. Literally, patterns are determined by the location of all the pieces (both yours and your opponent's) on the board in the present as well as the anticipated location of all the pieces in the future. It is the increasing control over pattern-making that best describes Thinking VI. This is pattern-making that responds to objectives that are known beforehand – like the objective in a game like chess.

Thinking VI gives children added flexibility. They can "think through" more than one solution to a problem, discarding solutions that are less "elegant" or that simply will not work. Richard was given a Thinking VI task like this:

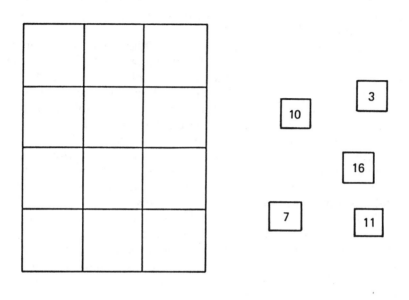

Fig. 10
Thinking VI task

The materials were comprised of a piece of cardboard divided into several squares along with a large pile of cardboard chips, each with a number on it. Richard was told that the object of the game was to fill up all the squares with numbers so as to get as close to a total of 40 as possible. Since there were more chips with numbers than there were empty squares to put them in, Richard had to decide which numbers would yield a total closest to 40. Richard made several discoveries along the way. For example, he chose two chips with the numbers 16 and 10 on them. After checking the total of these numbers with Lauraine he came to the conclusion that those numbers were too large to use on his board which happened to have twelve squares. He decided he couldn't find enough chips with very small numbers to fill up all the squares and even come close to a total of 40. He tried again by putting numbers in the squares one row at a time. Since Richard still has a few problems adding numbers, he checked out the total of each row with Lauraine before moving to the next one. If he thought the total for a row was too high for the number of squares that were left, he substituted one or more chips for ones with lower numbers.

It is clear that Richard was able to use Thinking VI. However, he is not very sophisticated in this kind of thinking. He does not for example try to organize the chips into groups totalling 40 independently of the board. This would be difficult for him since he requires help adding the numbers. On the other hand, Richard is able to *make patterns* with the numbers because he understands that there is a relationship between the parts and the whole, e.g., that the chips can't give you a high number too quickly or all the squares won't be used up when the chips total 40. In other words, he understands that there is a relationship between the entire set of squares and the growing total contained in a sub-set of these squares.

We should note that Richard's flexibility can also be found in the use he makes of the resource person (the adult) who is sharing this situation with him. He does not hesitate to use the adult's expertise when it is appropriate to do so. An analogous situation might occur for adults when a very large number (as a stated objective in this task) might require the use of an aid like a calculator.

## Thinking VII Tasks

Thinking VII makes it possible for children to understand metaphorical or figurative meaning. To do this they must detect a similarity between ideas, objects or events that sometimes belong in different domains. For example we could show children a picture of a violin, a tree and a singing-canary and ask which pictures go together. They might say that the violin and the tree go together because they are wood. These children would not be demonstrating metaphorical understanding although clearly these things are similar on the basis of physical resemblance, e.g., they are both made of wood. However, should children put the violin and singing-canary together we would say they are demonstrating metaphorical understanding because they are putting together things from quite different category domains where there is no physical resemblance between the pictures. These children must make a metaphoric "leap" to put these pictures together. This kind of "conceptual leaping" is especially important for learning potential because it describes thinking that is fundamental to generalizing; applying old learning in a new situation (e.g., where violins and canaries are compared). Children will have a more elaborated understanding of both violins and canaries when they are able to describe how these things are similar.

Metaphorical thinking is even more flexible than Thinking VI. Whereas Thinking VI makes it possible for children to generate several different solutions to a given problem or for example give many different uses for objects like bricks, Thinking VII makes it possible for children to identify a problem where none had been perceived before or to relate as in the example above, a hard brick to something in a completely different conceptual domain. Many children Richard's age will understand, "The jail guard's muscles are bricks." These children are being *creative* in the kinds of comparisons they make and consequently in the kinds of ideas that emerge from these comparisons. They have moved from responding to problems that have been stated beforehand and pattern making using old rules in different ways, to problem identification and the invention of new rules for manipulating symbols.

Richard was given the metaphoric triads task (MTT) developed by Kogan, Connor, Gross and Fava (1980); the questions are our own:

|     |     |     |
| :-: | :-: | :-: |
|  1  |  2  |  3  |

Find *two* pictures that go together the best.
Which two pictures do you think they are? — and —
Why do you think they go together?
Find *two* pictures that go together *second* best.
Which two pictures do you think they are? — and —
Why do you think they go together?

Fig. 11
Metaphoric triads task

The MTT is comprised of 29 items one of which (violin, singing-canary, tree) was described above. Some similarities are within the surface properties of the pictures themselves (winding-river, snake) while others are more conceptual requiring children to transform the pictures into their symbolic referents in order to appreciate the similarity between them (old man, candle-nearly-burned-down). Pictures in the MTT can always be related on a nonmetaphoric basis, for example the smoke from the candle and the smoking pipe. Richard made metaphoric connections for 17 of the 29 items on the MTT. He was able to justify his pairings on the basis of the conceptual relationship between the pictures. These results show that Richard is beginning to use Thinking VII which means he is becoming capable of the kind of concept elaboration we described above.

Richard was given another kind of task to assess Thinking VII. This is a proverb task developed by Gamlin and his colleagues (Gamlin & Tramposch, 1981; Djap, 1983). Here is an example:

Proverb: *You cannot eat your cake and keep it too*
Sometimes you can do only one of two things
You can eat your cake and ask for more
You can either eat your cake or keep it
Sometimes you can do everything that you want to do

Fig. 12
Proverb task

Richard was asked to do two things. First, to check off two sentences that "mean about the same as the proverb". Second, of these two sentences, to check off one that he thought was "the very best meaning" of the proverb. As with the MTT it is possible to select the nonproverbial sentence; one that does not require a "conceptual leap". We gave Richard 10 items from the 30 item proverb test. In seven of the ten items Richard was able to select the sentence that paraphrased the moral of the proverb. Furthermore, he thought it was the better sentence, that really "gave the best meaning of the proverb".

# Summing Up Richard's Assessment

The results for Thinking I through VII suggest that Richard is developmentally advanced with respect to similarity thinking skills. These results therefore strongly support the view that he has considerable potential to learn.

## *Implications for the Home and School*

Throughout this book we have suggested that teachers will more effectively respond to individual needs when they organize their perceptions and activities around the central concept of learning potential. Part of this perspective means that they will need to focus on the child's personal best in the context of the development of similarity thinking. In addition, we want to encourage teachers and school system staff to go beyond assessment results and classroom performance in order to incorporate information from the home and in this way to get "the big picture". Although assessment results like the ones we report in this chapter for Richard are important, we want to stress that these results should be interpreted in the context of Richard as a whole person.

## *Networking or Systems Approach*

We suggest that the teacher is the most appropriate person to coordinate these different kinds of information. Indeed we would argue that this is the single most important function of the teacher, since an understanding of the child's potential to learn and the development of this potential is fundamental to content mastery. In chapter eight we elaborate upon the networking approach but first we need to discuss the implication of this assessment for Richard's emotional development. We do this in the next chapter to demonstrate how emotional and cognitive development go together. We make specific recommendations to Richard's parents and school system staff.

# Chapter 7

# Therapy for The "Sane" Child

In the last chapter we saw at least three different pictures of Richard. We saw him through the eyes of the school system staff, through his parent's eyes and from the perspective of the similarities thinking assessment. But even after all of these snap-shots we still do not have a complete picture of the flesh and blood Richard; the emotional Richard; the seven and one-half-year old, little boy, Richard.

He is enthusiastic, once he learns that he can trust you. His enthusiasm is reflected in his chatter which is full of observation and humour. For example, one day he was with the author's wife in the cafeteria when they were joined by a man named Peter. Richard's response was, "You (Lauraine) have a Peter. I have a Peter. And here is another Peter. What are we going to do with all these Peters?" A few weeks later he came back to this saying, "It's all very confusing with all of these Peters! I can't just use the name Peter and expect that you'll know which one I mean!"

On another occasion Lauraine and Richard were working together and Richard was constantly making moves toward the water fountain. The first time he was encouraged to get a drink of water but after that he pestered for more. He finally left for the fountain without permission and without paying heed to the requests to return. When he finally did return, Lauraine was part-way out the door. Richard ran behind asking what she was doing, where she was going and why she had left without him. When she didn't respond, Richard in a very emotional sentence said "I know you are not listening to me now because I didn't listen to you!" At this point he grabbed Lauraine's hand and made eye-contact with her to make sure she paid attention to him. Since Richard is normally a very tactile person, physical contact is always natural and spontaneous.

Contrasting with the lively outspoken Richard, the Richard with the rich array of cognitive skills described in the last chapter, is the Richard that refuses to speak with people he does not like, even when they make special efforts to get close to him. Lauraine asked him about this one day and he replied seriously, "It's my life." Richard persisted with this explanation even when the sometimes dysfunctional consequences were pointed out to him as, for example, getting along in the classroom.

Richard's demonstrations of independence are often dysfunctional because they generate a negative response from others, usually directed at both him and the adult he is with. For example, one morning after a sesssion Richard asked if he could spend a little more time with Lauraine. Since she had some banking to do it was a good opportunity to see how he would respond in that situation. He was given a pencil and some paper to occupy himself while he was waiting. The paper was transformed into a number of airplanes which tested out the air currents given off by the ventilation system in the bank. At the same time he carried on a loud one-way conversation with Lauraine from across the room. Upon leaving the bank he remarked, "I bet the people in the bank thought you were my mother and were just waiting for you to punish me because I wasn't doing what I was supposed to be doing!" Richard's behaviour in this situation is dysfunctional because he knew that he was responsible for a lot of negative reaction that he was sharing with Lauraine. For him, this clown-behaviour was a means to "humour", thereby establishing his "independence" and his individuality. It certainly guaranteed that he would receive considerable attention. It also tells us that Richard is experiencing a crisis of confidence. In our view, this kind of behaviour is an indication that Richard is an insecure and highly anxious person, particularly in these kinds of situations. Richard's clown-behaviour is a mask covering up his true feelings. There is no way he wants to hurt Lauraine by making the situation unpleasant for her. We shall return to Richard's crisis of confidence but first we turn to an approach that seems to be working for him.

Considering all of these snap-shots of Richard, most probably you would agree that he is "sane" no matter what definition you might use to define the word. On the other hand, he most certainly is not succeeding at school and he does not seem to be able to bring to bear the most positive qualities of his personality in many situations including the classroom situation. It is in this sense that Richard needs "therapy" because he is only a step away from calling himself a "shit-head".

There are at least ten Richards in every grade and in every class of 30 children. They span the entire range of potential to learn. These are youngsters in regular classrooms being taught by regular teachers. Therapy for these "sane" Richards involves assessing their potential to learn as well as reassuring them that they are not alone.

Richard needs to understand that most of us never seem to achieve completely our human potential. We strive, but in the striving become increasingly aware of the discrepancy between what we wish we were and what we are. As adults, we explain this kind of discrepancy in a variety of ways. We may speak of good intentions, deficiencies in character and missed opportunities. We may indulge in even more blatant scape-goating, blaming our ethnic or economic background, our poor education, or the state of the economy.

The important point is not that we invariably make excuses for our behaviour, but rather that we are always conscious of the discrepancy between what we think it is possible for us to achieve and the reality of our day to day activities. We often talk of lost dreams and unfulfilled ambitions. The positive side of this is that the very act of becoming conscious of the discrepancy between our dreams and the reality of our daily lives makes it possible for us to see more clearly our potential for the future. If we choose to tackle this "mission impossible", we must learn where our skills are lacking and where our vision is off the mark. It is essential to understand our potential and our limitations. At this juncture, as sensible or "sane" adults, we may look for help in some form of therapy not so much to fix something that has broken but rather to learn how to realize more of our potential. We seek reassurance that our vision has some validity, that our skills are retrievable, that we can still learn. This may, in part, explain why so many adults in or approaching middle age, return to university, or make an attempt to change jobs.

The discrepancy between desire and achievement is a phenomena that seems to be universal in this species human. It is important to realize that this also applies to children and especially to our Richards. Youngsters do have a "vision" of what is possible. They have perception. They can visualize or "see-into". For example, the three-year old who throws a blanket over a clothesline creates something that he calls a house. Clearly this child knows that there is a difference between a real house and the house of his imagination. He has exercised his vision of the possible and in so doing has expanded his entire notion of what a house is all about. The child has "personalized" a concept, in this case, "house". Even though the child could not build a real house, brick by brick, he can use his imagination to create a house, using clothes line and blanket. This house is personal because it is his very own. In the same way a child may imagine herself to be a queen. She may then expand this concept by making a crown out of cardboard. This is a very personal concept of queen because it is her own. In this way these children have gone beyond accepted meanings for house and queen and in so doing have expanded their own ideas. They have done so by exercising their vision of what is possible. We see here the roots of the child's use of metaphor (this blanket is a house). Even very young children can think metaphorically although their metaphors are very simple and intuitive.

Average children have ripe imaginations: they appreciate the phantasmagorical. Nevertheless, they are always ready to remark upon the difference between the imagined and the real. Children's vision of what is possible or what can be imagined makes their behaviour very electric and robust in the early stages of their development. We have all noticed the spontaneity of our average or "sane" children. This spontaneity seems to reflect how much confidence these children bring to their activities, a confidence which comes from their belief in a vision of what is possible; in their ability to learn and in their ability to achieve what they have imagined. It is the child's imagination that acts as a stimulus for achievement. Our "sane" Richard will be able to coordinate the real and the imagined by noticing that they are different and then take action aimed at what is possible.

When we attempt to realize our potential to learn we are probably trying to understand what is possible. Unfortunately for many children and adults, the role of the imagination has been banished to the realm of fantasy instead of being fostered as an important part of the learning process. For example, the use of imagination in schools is largely seen to be dysfunctional. We often hear the following refrains: "Your child will not pay attention, Mrs. Jones" or "Your child seems to want to escape into fantasy, Mrs. Jones" or "Your child is a day-dreamer, Mrs. Jones." However, when we come to understand that imagination is just one end of the "reality" continuum, we will see that children will want to coordinate what is real with what is imagined because that is their starting point for learning what it is possible for them to accomplish. If the relationship between reality and imagination is interrupted, children will begin to lose confidence, will begin to stifle their spontaneity and will lose sight of what they want to achieve.

This is when special help for the "sane" child can be most effective. Interestingly, getting high marks and having high levels of learning potential is no guarantee that youngsters are not losing their ability to take note of what is possible. We all know that memorizing facts may yield satisfactory grades but not necessarily understanding. What is required is a re-kindling of the original dialogue between what is real and what can be imagined. If youngsters seems to have lost interest in learning it may be because they have lost sight of their purpose for learning. They have lost their goals. These youngsters are usually not succeeding at school. Like the rational or "sane" adult, they are aware of a discrepancy between what they would like to achieve and

94

what they are actually achieving from day to day. They want their grades to be better. And like many adults, these children often come to feel lost or alienated and see themselves as losers. Instead of focusing on what is real and what is imagined so as to understand what is possible they focus on their problems, especially such things as the difference between their grades and the grades of the other children in their classroom. They do not have a concept of "personal best" because they have lost sight of what is possible for them.

Fortunately, youngsters like Richard usually have a well-developed sense of humour which is a potent source of energy because it is so natural and honest. Often the most important first step in helping these children is to reassure them that it is perfectly all right to laugh, even – and this is a crucial breakthrough – at themselves. This seems to help children get a proper perspective of themselves as worthwhile persons. We sometimes achieve this goal through mime, by exaggerating the seriousness of the expression and pointing to the mask and to the clown that lies just beneath the mask. The trying on of different masks makes most children laugh while at the same time it points to flexibility and to the possibility for change. Using this approach even our "class clowns" can be helped to gain some perspective, to see the implication of their being the brunt of their own jokes. "Hey Richard, you wear a tee-shirt with a message printed on it that says: I'm a Fool."

Although laughter is not an easy first step, it is fundamental. Once this source of energy is opened up by using humour, we begin to reintroduce children to the dialogue between what is real and what can be imagined. We do this by using educational toys, enabling children to have direct hands-on experience, immediately succeeding on tasks which require coordinating reality (the materials) with imagination (the innovative ways they use the materials). In our experience it is only a short step from these activities to the re-emergence of confidence, to the vision of what is possible, to accepting the challenge presented by the difference between the real and the imagined. Children will quickly understand that learning skills require development. For example, they may discover that it is useful to be able to read instructions. They will begin to understand the purpose for learning and in so doing regain their desire to learn.

Therapy for these children requires that instruction be provided in basic skill areas such as reading, writing and mathematics. The significant point is that youngsters will want to acquire these skills because they will understand why these skills are important. They will understand how they can use these skills to improve their "personal best". In this way we remind youngsters that these basic skills are not ends in themselves. We point out, for example, that learning how to read is a tool that can be used to explore various possibilities for using toy materials or exploring new worlds of experience through books. This leads in turn to writing, which again is a tool that can be used to express one's growing comprehension of what is possible. And so the cycle turns in upon itself, self-generating and functionally autonomous. This is the true sense of "learning how to learn". Children will understand that their purpose for learning is to exercise their vision of what is possible and so doing understand how to improve their personal best.

In the final stages of therapy for the "sane" child, exercises are used that help to stretch the child's imagination. Here we demonstrate the importance of metaphor and creative problem solving for seeing the world and one's experience through fresh eyes. We point out that there is more to being human than the ability to adapt or to survive the pressures which are a part of living day to day. We can do more than simply cope or get by.

We point out to our Richards that as members of the human species we are uniquely able to respond creatively to our environment and are able to make more than serendipitous or random gestures towards developing novel solutions to old problems. Indeed we are able to understand old problems in completely new ways by redefining them, seeing them in a different "light" in order to find unique and original solutions. Amazingly, this is done by transcending our "current consensus reality", just as the children described above expanded their ideas of "house" and "queen". We learn the importance of metaphor in our experience and in so doing understand our experience in a really different way. Richard, for example, might begin his adventure into metaphor by relating his failing grades to a dog straining at the end of his chain (my grades are a dog straining at the end of his chain). At that moment Richard begins to understand his problem in a new way. He will understand that he must break the chain holding back his potential to learn. He will acquire a new meaning for personal best. He then must be helped to move through a series of similar metaphors until he comes upon practical solutions to his problem. These metaphors will undoubtly be related to the fact of his distractibility.

The role of humour in therapy for these children is fundamental. It can be found in the kind of "reality-testing" that "sane" children or adults constantly apply to the world about them. One of the ways this kind of "reality-testing" will be found is in the appreciation of well-done satire. Good satire requires the kind of reasoning that makes it possible to move backwards and forwards between the real and the imagined. "Sane" children and adults never lose sight of the difference between the real and the imagined. They put on hold, all dictionary descriptions of the world. These people are in an ideal position to add to the dictionary words and meanings that they invent. We see this being done with the marvelous inventive imagination often used in poetry, in advertising and even in graffiti. It is this kind of reasoning that makes it possible to understand and see through the pretentious and ridiculous, to understand the necessity for exploring the unknown through free-ranging imagination. Clearly, there are some who will not be able to do this because thay are not exercising the kinds of thinking that make this possible. How many of us have sat uncomprehendingly through "Monty Python", "Saturday Nite Live" or "SCTV"? How many have heard remarks like, "I just don't see what's funny" or "That show is just so silly"? This kind of refrain may be indicative of a breakdown in the dialogue between the real and the imagined. It would seem that a good many people who make these kinds of remarks have almost completely shut down the process whereby they learn how to learn what is possible. They have lost the ability to stretch their imagination. They have regressed to a kind of concrete thinking that holds them mired in the muck of the ordinary.

As we have seen in the last chapter, Richard has all of the cognitive skills he will need to use his imagination to shuttle back and forth between the reality of his classroom performance and the range of possibilities (e.g., higher grades) that will be his when he exercises his potential to learn. We have suggested a means to achieve that end in this chapter. One of the most important outcomes of this approach is that Richard will have a more complete appreciation of the meaning of "personal best" in that he will understand that learning how to learn always is personal and that it always leads to the expanding horizon of what is possible.

## Crisis of Confidence Revisited

Richard is a boy who looks like he has all kinds of confidence. He seems to act independently and, in fact, he uses language like, "It's my life," to suggest that he is indeed autonomous. Furthermore, he refuses to interact with anyone he doesn't like. This, combined with his public display of clown-behaviour, tends to set him apart, as well as cause his teacher to throw up her hands in exasperation.

However, we have also seen that there is another side to Richard. When he comes to *trust* you he is warm and responsive and very willing to interact on the basis of the extremely broad range of cognitive skills that were described in the last chapter. He can be constructively entertaining when he uses his vivid imagination and humour to make an observation that we adults might simply take for granted.

## Erikson's Theory of Psychosocial Development

We have emphasized the word trust because this is a key to unlocking Richard's problem. Erik Erikson's (1963) theory of psychosocial development is particularly important to our understanding because developing a sense of trust over mistrust is the first of eight stages of psychosocial development. In order to understand why this is so important, it is necessary to appreciate a few significant aspects of Erikson's theory. Erikson believed that the ego develops in response to the demands of society. These demands change as the child gets older. The ego must adapt to these changing demands by acquiring new ego capacities since each new societal demand requires a different adaptation by the ego. For Erikson, the ego develops these new capacities because there is a maturational timetable that is a part of development. Erikson calls this timetable an *epigenetic principle.* As defined by Erikson, "... this principle states that anything that grows has a ground plan, and that out of this ground plan the parts arise, each having its time of special ascendancy, until all parts have arisen to form a functioning whole" (1959, p. 52). On this view, the child has only a limited time to develop each stage-specific capability. Time is limited because the timetable of development will move on to the next stage of development, irrespective of whether or not the necessary capability was developed. Thus, each stage of psychosocial developement is a critical period. For healthy ego development to proceed, the emotional crisis which is part of each stage must be successfully resolved. If it is not, the rest of development will be unfavorably altered. When all parts of the whole (ego) should have arisen to form one synthesized, functioning whole, the person will be lacking the completed, or adequate, development of an ego part, an ego capability.

Erikson describes eight types of ego capabilities, the first four of which are particularly important for Richard. The first emotional crisis confronting the infant is to make some sense of, or incorporate, the vast array of sensory information that arises from the social world. In this *oral-sensory* stage, the child experiences the sensory world in some degree of pleasant toward unpleasant. The infant's experience may be mostly benign, or mostly negative or harsh, or in some degree between these polar extremes. If the infant has relatively pleasant sensory experiences, then the infant will feel that the world is supportive and safe. This infant will develop a sense of trust. If, on the other hand, the experience is painful and creates discomfort, the infant will develop a sense of mistrust. The emotional crisis, then, is between *trust versus mistrust.*

Erikson is very careful to point out that complete trust or complete mistrust is unadaptive. The individual who has complete trust would always look to others to take care of him while the person who mistrusts would feel that assuredly the world will hurt him. For Erikson, then, for successful resolution of this emotional crisis, trust must always be greater *in some degree* than mistrust. We want to stress that there is a continuum of possibilities between trust and mistrust because we shall return to this point below. For now, it is important to understand that degree of trust/over mistrust describes the extent to which the appropriate ego capacity has been developed and consequently how ready or prepared the child is for the next stage of psychosocial development.

Erikson describes the second crisis as involving the child's capability of being able to control his overall bodily movements. In this *anal-musculature* stage, the child either experiences a kind of helplessness because he cannot do things for himself that both he and others feel he should be doing for himself or he feels effective in the mastery of these movements. Therefore, the second psychosocial crisis is one between *autonomy versus shame and doubt.* Once again autonomy must always be greater than shame and doubt, in some degree, for successful resolution of this emotional crisis and the attendant development of the appropriate ego capacity.

The third emotional crisis revolves around the child's ability to make use of his own movements to break away from a strict dependency on mother. When the child is able to act on his own without proddings from his parents, he will develop a sense of initiative. If the child remains dependent upon the parents, especially the mother, he will experience guilt. In this *genital-locomotor* stage, it is the degree of *initiative/over guilt* that characterizes successful ego development and resolution of the third emotional crisis.

The fourth emotional crisis turns around the child responding to those tasks necessary for being adult members of society. In our society this means that the child is sent off to school. When the child succeeds at school he experiences a sense of accomplishment in that he learns what to do and how to do it. For Erikson, this means he has developed a sense of industry. The child who does not succeed at school will experience a sense of inferiority because he will perceive that others have capably performed the requisite tasks of his society. In this *latency* stage, it is the degree of *industry/over inferiority* which resolves the fourth emotional crisis and develops the appropriate ego capacity.

Erikson's theory of psychosocial development is summarized below:

| *Psychosocial stage* | *Emotional crisi* | |
|---|---|---|
| 1. Oral-sensory | basic trust | – mistrust |
| 2. Anal-musculature | autonomy | – shame, doubt |
| 3. Genital-locomotor | initiative | – guilt |
| 4. Latency | industry | – inferiority |
| 5. Puberty and adolescence | identity | – role confusion |
| 6. Young adulthood | intimacy | – isolation |
| 7. Adulthood | generativity | – stagnation |
| 8. Maturity | ego integrity | – despair |

Since we want to focus on Richard, we have outlined only four of Erikson's stages. It is probably evident that Erikson is describing the development of self-sufficiency, not in the sense of behaviour which diverges from societal expectations but rather in the sense of behaviour which is in correct concert *with* society. This kind of self-sufficiency requires that individuals experience a supportive and safe world within which they are free to develop the social and cognitive skills that give rise to independent action (again within the context of societal demands). We see the consequence of independent action and developing self-sufficiency in each psychosocial stage. We see it when the adolescent discovers his or her uniqueness in the context of society as a whole (stage 5, identity); in the capacity for intimacy (stage 6); in productivity (stage 7); and in the celebration of accomplishment (stage 8).

Before we return to Richard, we must describe the security theory of William Blatz (1944) because this theory offers an excellent interface between Erikson's psychosocial stages and the kind of therapy we have prescribed for the "sane" child.

# The Security Theory of William Blatz

Blatz was convinced that there was a relationship between feelings of security, our ability to take on responsibilities, and the way we learn. On this view:

> Security may defined as the state of consciousness which accompanies a willingness to accept the consequences of one's own decisions and actions. Only thus can an individual feel comfortably adjusted to his environment. This concept of security is dynamic, for man's adjustment can never become static. Any attempt on the part of the individual to maintain the status quo is ineffective, because life is a continuous process and man's security is based on the future, not on the present nor on the past. It is unfortunate that in our language there is no term to distinguish security as here described from the common meaning of security which implies safety. Safety is the antithesis of this type of security. An individual seeks to be secure and must continue his search, for as soon as he stops he becomes insecure (Blatz, 1944, p. 165).

For Blatz the willingness to accept the consequences of one's own decisions and actions, on an ongoing basis, can be achieved only when individuals move from dependency on others, what he called a "dependent security" relationship, to a more autonomous relationship where personal decision making and action are distinct possibilities. This kind of autonomy will, in turn, open-out the possibility for what Blatz called feelings of "independent security":

> Independent security can be attained only in one way – by the acquisition of a skill through learning. Whenever an individual is presented with a situation for which he is inadequately prepared, or whenever he is striving for something and finds that his preparation is inadequate, he must make one of two choices – he must either retreat or attack. This situation is emotionally charged. But there is more than the emotional content in such situations. The individual must, if he is to attack, emerge from the state of dependent security and accept the state of insecurity. This attack, of course, will result in learning. The degree of skill which he acquires will depend upon his persistence. But once having learned, he will meet this situation in the future with assurance, because now he possesses a behaviour pattern which makes it possible for him to adapt himself satisfactorily. Furthermore, he has become familiar with the consequences of his advance and is willing to face them. (Blatz, 1944, p. 167)

101

Blatz continues:

> The individual, through his efforts, learns that satisfaction results from overcoming the apprehension and anxiety experienced when insecure, and that he may reach a state of independent security through learning. He develops a habit of accepting *insecurity* as the only way towards independent security. Having once experienced independent security, he learns that he may continue in this state only if he continues to learn more and more, because learning itself exposes the need for further learning. (Blatz, 1944, p. 167)

Blatz observed that most individuals are not willing to make the effort towards becoming independently secure. In large part this is so because, especially in early childhood, there are few occasions where independent action leads to consequences that must be faced and "owned" by the child. On this view the child must frequently say to him or herself, "I did this, and this is what happened. Do I want this to happen?" The child must experience the consequences of his actions:

> Responsibility may be defined as the habit of choosing, and accepting the consequences of the choice of behaviour. Whenever a child is considered to have developed or acquired sufficient experiences in anticipating the consequences of his acts, he should be expected to accept these consequences. If this behaviour shows that he *cannot* do so, then the opportunity for choice should be deliberately withdrawn. If, on the other hand, his behaviour is interpreted as an *unwillingness* to accept the consequences, then responsibility should not be withdrawn. (Blatz, 1944, pp. 187–188)

For example, occasions for eating occur frequently. These occasions can become learning experiences. Very young children, as Blatz observes, cannot be expected to decide *when* to eat or *what* to eat. "These responsibilities rest with the parent, and cannot be delegated to the child ..." Children, however, may choose *whether* they will eat or will not eat upon any particular occasion – but then they must live with the consequences. Furthermore, as children develop and acquire more autonomy and feelings of independent security even the when and what of eating must be open to personal decision and consequent responsibility for that decision.

For parents, watching this kind of development and experiencing the child trying to sort all of this out, the temptation is to step in and "help", not only because they want to make it "easier" for the child but because it takes up a lot of time and uses up a considerable amount of patience to see Blatz's recommendations through. However, consider the alternative. When parents "step in to help", they are taking away the child's opportunity to act independently and consequently they are taking away any responsibility the child might have developed for that action. The parents become what Blatz called *deputy agents*. The child becomes dependent on these agents and hence the only security the child knows is *dependent security*. The deputy agent accepts the responsibility for the consequences of the child's actions rather than the child.

On Blatz's account, because this is such a difficult exercise, children mostly adopt deputy agents, rather than making an effort toward independent security through learning. This is

> ... the commonest technique used by an individual for avoiding the immediate effort necessary to achieve independent security. If he uses a deputy agent only as a temporary expedient which he recognizes as such, no harm arises; but if he persists in using it to solve the same problem again and again, then it becomes a mentally unhealthy device. (Blatz, 1944, p. 170)

For Blatz, the use of deputy agents to reduce feelings of insecurity has a consequence for the entire life-span. It is not necessary to understand the Freudian terminology in the following table (Blatz, 1944, p. 171) to understand how wide-spread is our use of deputy agents.

There is one further point to make about this theory before we return to Erikson and therapy for the sane child. Blatz believed that a certain degree of dependent security and consequently a certain reliance on deputy agents was a developmentally prior and a necessary precursor to independent security and the acceptance of personal responsibility. Healthy development is impossible when the child is in a state of insecurity. Dependent security is the first step away from insecurity and in that sense it "paves the way" for independent security. Remember that for Blatz independent security is always accompanied by anxiety, because the individual never knows exactly what to expect (as a consequence) or whether his preparation is adequate. Therefore he must develop "a habit of accepting *insecurity* as the only way toward independent security". In order to deal with this kind of insecurity the individual must have already experienced feelings of security even though they may have been tied to the actions of deputy agents. Without an adequate foundation of dependent security the individual would never be able to take the risks associated with taking independent and responsible action, associated as it is with the

## Description of Types of Behaviour Employed
## to Avoid Sense of Insecurity

| Device for Deputy Agent | Child | | Adult | |
|---|---|---|---|---|
| | Healthy | Unhealthy | Healthy | Unhealthy |
| Substitution | Attachment to nurse, grand-mother, etc., siblings | "Playing off one parent against the other" "Using a toy as constant com-panion" | Companionship Religion | Bigotry |
| Rationalization | "When I grow up I will do thus and so" | "Sour grapes" | Logic is the saf-est form of rationalization | Excuses: "I have no time" "It isn't done" |
| Compensation | Accepts sub-missive roles | Spanks her dolls in play Bullying | "Hobbies" | Arrogance Snobishness Cruelty |
| Sublimation | Obeys rules in order to belong to group | Sulking | Sports | Hysteria Masochism |

anxiety and insecurity that comes out of not knowing what to expect. But once the risk has been taken and the individual begins to learn, "he will meet this situation in the future with assurance, because now he possesses a behaviour pattern which makes it possible for him to adapt himself satisfactorily. Furthermore, he has become familiar with the consequences of his advances and is willing to face them."

Blatz would seem to be suggesting that the child must experience two important developments before independent security can be achieved. The first has to do with establishing the kind of consistency that comes out of dependent security. In this context the child knows what to expect. The second development turns around experiencing the gradual relaxation of deputy agent expectations. In this context the child is given the opportunity to make independent choices and to accept the consequences of these choices. Parental behaviour is par-ticularly important here because the child must be reassured that this kind of autonomy is appropriate and valued. With these two develop-ments the individual achieves a state of independent security (learning that he is sufficiently able to handle the consequence of having taken a risk). Additionally, the individual understands "... that he may continue in this state only if he continues to learn more and more, because learning itself exposes the need for further learning."

## Erikson, Blatz and Therapy for the "Sane" Child

Both Erikson and Blatz describe how children become self-reliant in the context of societal demands. The individual with this kind of self-confidence exudes an attitude of "yes I can", "I'll try again" and "let me at it". This individual, for Erikson, has developed and continues to develop adaptive ego capacities in response to each of the emotional crises in each psychosocial stage. Erikson would seem to be in agreement with Blatz with respect to the child's need for feelings of dependent security early on (sense of trust/over mistrust) followed by gradual emancipation from the expectations of both parental and other types of deputy agents. The general thrust of this kind of development is similar to Maslow's process of "self-actualization" or Rogers' "on becoming a person" who is capable of "unconditional positive regard". In each of these theories of personality development, the concept of self becomes distinct within the context of society at large (sense of identity/over role confusion).

There would appear to be considerable consensus about how to describe the mental health of individuals who continue to adapt successfully throughout their life-span. These individuals are essentially free or independent enough, to be vulnerable to the anxieties attendent on new learning. For example, on Blatz's view, individuals will be able to embrace *insecurity* because this is the only route to learning something that is not already known. While these individuals may experience vulnerability at this point in the learning process they become stronger in the knowledge that the *means* to this knowledge was *unique* and stronger yet in the knowledge that it was also uniquely successful. In the language of therapy for the sane child we say that healthy or sane individuals focus on the discrepancy between the now of where they are and what they can imagine is a posssibility for them. They have a "vision" of what is possible and they take responsibility for moving toward it.

Importantly, healthy individuals do not attempt to realize their "vision" independently of others. They are capable of relating to others in an intimacy that is "game-free", to use the language of Eric Berne. They do not "throw expectancies at one another" (Fritz Perls).

105

Healthy individuals experience interpersonal relations in the same way that they employ the means to learn "what is possible". These individuals open-out to others and in so doing make themselves vulnerable to criticism. They become stronger in the realization that any response they receive, critical or not, is a response to a "cards on the table", authentic and intimate *me*. Even a negative response is at least a response to the real "me" and not a response to the "me" that may have been thrown up (like a mask) to appease someone else's expectations.

Healthy individuals offer no excuses for, or defense of, the self that is totally exposed in an intimate relationship. This is because these individuals are continuously learning about the self just as they continue to learn other things; "learning itself exposes the need for further learning". In this context healthy individuals focus on what is possible (a personal best self) and not on the frozen snapshot of another person's perceptions.

This "picture of mental health" cannot be achieved as an overnight phenomenon. Both Erikson and Blatz emphasize the importance of development in the acquisition of these learning skills. Children must acquire a state of dependent security before they are able to successfully respond to Erikson's emotional crises. They must practise accepting responsibility for their actions as they begin to experience a state of independent security. As children become more independent and more accepting of responsibility they are more able to tolerate the feelings of insecurity that go along with learning what is possible. And so it goes, success building on success, emotional crises surmounted one after the other. These individuals are learning how to trust in the future, to understand the expression, "the universe unfolds as it should", not in the fatalistic (do nothing and it will come about anyway) sense but rather in the sense of trusting in themselves to realize their vision of what is possible.

Therapy for the sane child "reviews" this kind of development and provides exercises to strengthen those feeling states that are out of "balance". For example, we might want to encourage a child to acquire a better balance of trust/over mistrust. To do this we would focus on the child's state of dependent security. We would identify deputy agents who would demand particular kinds of behaviour and do so consistently. Once this child has "built-up" a better balance of trust/over mistrust and consequently "built-up" a state of dependent security we move on to gradual autonomy and encourage the child to accept the consequences of his or her actions.

We must understand where the child is with respect to cognitive skills because we need a good match between the child's potential to learn and the "balancing" exercises. The theory of similarity thinking is particularly useful here because it provides a description of the kind of cognitive skills that seem to be necessary for learning how to learn – which is the single most outstanding achievement of the healthy individual. The assessment results therefore tell us to what extent these learning how to learn skills have developed. We are then able to match this kind of learning potential to the appropriate "balancing" exercises. In the final paragraphs of this chapter we describe what we recommend for Richard given the results of the cognitive skills assessment and our review of his mental health achievements.

Before we make specific recommendations for Richard, we present one more example of the kind of person he is. Following a session with Lauraine, both she and Richard proceeded to his father's office. His father is a dentist, and it was Lauraine's intention to make an appointment with him to have some work done. Although this would ordinarily only require some interaction with the receptionist, Richard decided that Lauraine should see his father. Richard persisted in interrupting him on three different occasions even though he was very busy with his clients and really had no time to see Lauraine. Finally, in exasperation Richard's father came out to see why Lauraine needed to see him. While she was pointing out that this was Richard's agenda and not hers, Richard was demanding in a loud voice from down the hall that Lauraine tell him how fantastic his reading was, how well he had done that day and generally about all of the good things that he had accomplished.

This more complete picture of Richard shows that he having difficulty responding to the emotional crisis found in Erikson's fourth psychosocial stage. Richard does not feel confident in his understanding of the skills he is expected to acquire at school. In Erikson's terms he seems to have a balance of inferiority/over industry. He is, however, fighting to shift this balance, as we observe in his overt crying out for reassurance from the person he trusts the most in the teaching situation. Richard also wants to show his father that he is on the right track, doing the right kinds of things and making significant progress. He wants to please his father and even more importantly, he wants to please himself.

From Blatz's perspective we see a boy who is not independently secure. Richard in his public displays of clown-behaviour and in his larger than life vocal interactions in public places is demonstrating that he is not always able to accept the consequences of his actions. This kind of inappropriate behaviour is indicative of the kind of anxiety Richard must experience as a consequence of his feelings of insecurity – particularly when he is expected to perform well at school.

Therapy for this very sane Richard involves reducing his feelings of insecurity by helping him rediscover and develop a state of dependent security. Richard must be exposed to deputy agents who make consistent, rule-based demands of him. In other words, at this time, his freedom of choice should be restricted. He should be told what to do as well as praised when he succeeds. Richard needs structure; he needs to be able to count on what is going to happen when he behaves in a certain way. The key word is consistency. Richard will begin to feel more secure when deputy agents are making decisions for him and doing so consistently. Because Richard has experienced freedom of choice he also needs the occasional opportunity to engage in independent decision making. He needs to experience the consequences of his actions so he can feel responsible for them.

Richard should continue to see Lauraine who has the training to decide whether Richard is ready for more independent decision making. She observes whether or not Richard can accept the consequences of his actions by giving him free rein to do so in the shelter of her office. Lauraine will encourage Richard to accept these consequences responsibly since this is the route to his being able to adapt to the insecurity that is a part of being independently secure.

Richard has all of the cognitive skills he will need to respond to the demands of the school. What he needs to do in the security of Lauraine's office is to focus on where he is in terms of his performance at school at the same time as he experiences the "vision" of what he would like to achieve. Exercising Richard's thinking skills by stimulating his imagination will reduce the discrepancy between where he is and his vision of what is possible. This kind of exercise will also encourage Richard to become independently secure in that the setting provides the vehicle for Richard to experience the insecurity of learning what is possible.

Richard's teacher and other school system staff must assume the role of deputy agents. They should help Richard become dependently secure by assuming most of the decision making for him. At this point in time Richard requires a lot of structure, where penalties and rewards are applied consistently. Richard's teacher and other school system staff must remain responsive to Lauraine's observations since they are the key to the gradual relaxation of this rather strict regimen of rules and regulations. Making this kind of determination requires that Lauraine consult with Richard's teacher as to his "readiness" for more independent behaviour since the teacher observes Richard over long periods of time and in a greater variety of situations. In all probability Richard will acquire a better balance of industry/over inferiority after only a few months, but only if this program is put in place and applied consistently.

We have observed from Richard's assessment that he is not a slow learner. However, he does need more practice with basic skills, and he needs this practice in the learning environment we have just described. We must stress that this environment should not be unpleasant. Discipline should be used matter-of-factly as if this is just the way it is, and no hard feelings.

In the next chapter we discuss some of the stumbling blocks that often get in the way of putting this kind of program into practice.

# Chapter 8

# The Frustration of Meeting the Individual Needs of Students

We begin this chapter with excerpts from a recent provincial (Ontario) Review Report (1983, Number 1) to put teachers' concerns into a broad perspective. We follow this with an interview with two teachers of grades 1 and 2. The chapter concludes with recommendations for teachers about how to talk to parents who have children with learning problems and more generally how to respond to the individual needs of students.

The report of the junior kindergarten, kindergarten, grade one task force was based on the professional judgements of seventeen reviewers from the Ministry of Education and the field who were highly experienced in Primary education. Teams of two or three spent up to three days in schools observing classrooms, talking with school staff, parents, social workers, in short, any individual who could shed light on the nurturing, educational, and developmental needs of young children.

The task force observed "pockets of excellence" scattered throughout the province but much that needed improvement. One area where improvement was warranted concerned early ongoing identification, to determine individual learning strengths and needs and to develop programs that enhance children's overall development.

> We found that the early and ongoing identification procedures in the schools we visited across the province reflect diverse philosophical views and practices. The procedures some school boards have adopted reflect the intent and spirit of Ministry policy and direction as outlined in Policy/Program Memorandum No. 11. These procedures include observing and assessing each child's general development, learning style, attitudes, personal and social characteristics, and talents. They also involve continuous program planning, monitoring, adjustment, and consultation among teachers and between parents and teachers.
>
> We consider the procedures of some school boards to be potentially harmful to young children, however. Some rely heavily on prepackaged programs and standardized tests which, in too many instances,

are inappropriate and restrictive. As a general observation, we found that too few programs incorporate the assessment information derived from the children's pre-school and in-school experiences. It was rare that classroom programs were modified to meet the needs of individual children. Instead, all children seem to be put through a predetermined program. This is particularly true in many Grade 1 classrooms where the only modification for accomodating the differences among six- and seven-year-olds is to move the child more slowly through the preset curriculum.

In some jurisdictions, a deficit or problem-search model of early screening is relied on, and only high-risk children receive programs that are adjusted to their needs. Sometimes these programs are designed, monitored, and adjusted by resource personnel working closely with classroom teachers.

In their desire to get to know each child as quickly as possible, some teachers conduct academic assessments before or shortly after the children enter Junior Kindergarten or Kindergarten. These assessments cover such areas as colour identification, language development, and numerical knowledge. We believe, however, that giving a series of tests to four- or five-year-olds before they feel secure in the school environment is not the best introduction to life in school.

The task force concluded their report with a significant observation concerning the differences between programs for J-K and Kindergarten as compared to those for Grade 1.

Within the schools, we found a marked discrepancy between the prevailing philosophies and practices for Junior Kindergarten and Kindergarten, and those for Grade 1. Some educators seem to believe that children grow up and grow old over the magical summer between Kindergarten and Grade 1. To borrow from George Bernard Shaw, we do not cease to play because we grow old, we grow old because we cease to play. In many schools, Kindergarteners are involved in open-ended, experiential, language-based programs. But down the hall in many of these same schools, a youngster who may be a year, a month, or only a day older, is confronted by programs that tend to revolve around far too much large-group instruction and teacher-directed, two-dimensional activity. In many Grade 1 classrooms, children are led through a pre-determined program.

Through early and ongoing identification prodedures, teachers accumulate much important information on the interests, needs. and capabilities of Junior Kindergarten, Kindergarten, and Grade 1 pupils. Although a few teachers use this information effectively to modify or personalize programs, others expressed a need for assistance in applying this information to program design. Co-operative planning among Junior Kindergarten, Kindergarten, Grade 1 teachers, and principals, was considered essential. A strong need was expressed for professional development activities, curriculum materials, and human resources to help principals and teachers develop the understanding and skills for creating positive and productive classroom programs for the youngest children in school.

It is hardly any wonder teachers need assistance in order to personalize and modify programs. Consider Richard's case from the previous two chapters. Here was a child who needed help early on but essentially what happened to him was that he was moved "more slowly through the preset curriculum". Was there an alternative open to his grade 1 and 2 teachers? The following interview summarizes some of the frustration these teachers must have experienced.


## Teachers Discuss the Frustration of Meeting the Individual Needs of Children

*Rosa:* "This is the kind of example (Richard) that is pretty common in grade 2. I taught a boy who really seemed to need extra help. He hadn't been identified in either Kindergarten or Grade 1. I brought the diagnostic and prescriptive teacher (dpt) in to assess the boy since she is the liaison between the teachers, special services people, like psychologists, and the board of education. She gave the boy two tests and he scored at about the 30th percentile. The dpt teacher was very supportive; she could see the boy really needed help. But what happened, the psychologist came along and said the boy would have to score below the 16th percentile before he could get help. There was no way that boy was going to learn in my class – I had over 30 kids to teach. Well I got very angry. The teacher gets no respect for her judgement about who needs help. Instead, everybody plays the numbers game and the children lose. I mean, I could show them that the boy wasn't retaining anything; he had no alphabet, no phonic skills; his printing was rudimentary, still pretty shaky. But no one would listen to me."

*Maria:* "I know what you mean. Many consultants tend to be patronizing. They focus on small details instead of offering constructive ideas for helping individual children. As teachers we have to go along with these consultants otherwise we lose all channels of communication with the administration."

*Rosa:* "What happens to people in every school board is that once they are promoted, they develop an inflated opinion of themselves.

113

They go from being a regular teacher to a consultant – to not talking to other teachers any more. All of a sudden from swearing at the system because thay may have 40 kids in their classroom, they start making ridiculous suggestions like: 'Why don't you make a book?' You know, 20 of the kids can't read but she says, 'Have you made a book?'"

*Maria:* "They have a limit to their knowledge yet they are in a position of absolute authority. It must be difficult and scary to have that much responsibility, to have an answer to every problem and to appear to be an expert."

*Rosa:* "Let me give you another example of kids having trouble learning. I worked for four years at a school that had a lot of transient kids. They would come in for a couple of months; then leave. Some would stay two years or so, go back to the West Indies – then return again. In that school they never had a grade 1 class smaller than 36 kids. Half of them were new Canadians and I'd end up referring ten of them. The principal and consultants would tell me – no they are six, they're immature, they're this, they're that – so I said what am I going to do with them? When I started teaching grade 1, I thought failing was a good idea. But because of the system, I've gone to the opposite end. I'd say, pass the kid because if he doesn't get two years behind – he won't be looked at."

*Maria:* "As a grade 1 teacher you really can't be sure what the cause of the child's inability to cope with the program really is. I had one child who didn't seem to care about reading and doing his work. I couldn't really fail him. I thought he had potential. So then his grade 2 teacher came to me and said why did you send him to me? He's not ready for grade 2. Anyway she failed him at the end of grade 2. Our principal has found a solution for the child who is not quite ready for grade 1. He has them put in grade 1 in the morning and kindergarten in the afternoon. This should work quite well except that these kids have to repeat grade 1 the year after anyway. It must be very frustrating for the child to go from kindergarten to grade 1 and not be ready for it. Maybe it would be better for everyone if they simply repeated kindergarten. But then of course you can run into problems with the parents who want their child in a full-day program since they both may be working, or as was the case for one family I know, they couldn't see the value of kindergarten. They thought their child would be just playing for another year.

"Smaller class sizes might give us more opportunity to tell whether a child is ready for grade 1 or 2. But we are always looking for what the child can do and not how he goes about trying to do it. We see whether children can print the right way; whether they can do the

114

arithmetic problems. We don't even begin to look at things like; do they use classification; can they use thinking skills of one kind or another. Instead of looking at the process of learning, we look at the end product. It's a pass-fail mentality with nothing in between. As a teacher of sometimes 25 – 30 children you don't have the time or the knowledge to find out whether you're getting at things more basic or necessary. Another fundamental problem of our school system is that teachers are overworked doing menial tasks. They are required to put up bulletin boards, sweep under sandtables, change water in paint jars, assist children to dress and undress, run-off dittos, supervise yard, bus and lunch duties, etc. These time-consuming responsibilities are inefficient uses of the teacher's training and expertise. As an example, I estimate that in the winter, I spend about 80 minutes of the school day assisting children with their outdoor wear. Having studied in university for five years and receiving a healthy wage, I think my time and knowledge could be better utilized individualizing programs, making uninterrupted observations, setting up activities or doing some of the planning, research, and marking that teachers do at home every evening.

"An assistant, such as a paraprofessional, knowledgeable about children but not necessarily as well-educated nor as highly paid as a teacher, could be freeing the teacher to perform his or her professional duties. This point became apparent to me on my last trip to the hairdresser: a secretary made my appointment, an assistant (probably an apprentice) shampooed my hair and another assistant swept the floor after the haircutting. The 'professional' hairdresser's talents were taken full advantage of. This example extends easily to many other professional office situations.

"Maybe, if all teachers, especially in the primary grades, were assigned assistants, they would value the important aspects of their teaching duties and burn-out would occur less frequently. In addition, the children could benefit from the added attention of another individual. The child's cognitive, social, affective and caretaking needs would be better satisfied by the teachers complementing each other's talents and training.

"Teachers would become more self-respecting and their positions would be held in higher esteem by the public, too. Of course, money comes into the picture – how would we pay for these assistants? I believe it could be done in either of two ways. Larger classrooms could be possible with the help of able assistants, or I think, some conscientious teachers would even take a moderate cut in pay to have more time and energy to better serve the needs of each child."

*Rosa:* "I guess if I were going to change the way things are now, I'd like a little more respect for the teacher from everybody. The parents are actually no problem. I've never had a problem with parents and I've taught in three different areas with children from three different ethnic backgrounds. What is really frustrating is when I approach the office and speak to the principal or whoever is my immediate superior and I'm told (and this is January and I know my kids) it may be maturation, a maturity thing. You know, by now I think I know how to pick out the maturity problems. The teacher's opinion always seems to need checking out by someone else. I can take six months to try to convince someone that a child needs help but it often requires no more than 10 minutes of the consultant's time with the child to get some action. In any case if that's what it takes at least come in and spend 20 minutes with the child right away and not six months later. Don't tell me without seeing the child that it is immaturity or something. It doesn't do either me or the child any good for the principal to say, have you tried this or that. I wouldn't be talking to him if I hadn't done those things already. I wonder, how many things do I have to do before you believe me?

"I'm not sure how teachers can get more respect. It's a bureaucratic thing. You have to go through so many channels before you can get where you want to be. The other alternative is to get the parents to make a fuss. But if the parents don't speak English, they don't understand what their rights are. And so they say – well, you do whatever is best.

"Maybe if all teachers had some kind of training in minor testing, the consultants wouldn't have to do it. The consultant could give whoever needed it, a more detailed one that required more training. Maybe that way people would start listening to teachers and teachers would be able to really talk to consultants.

"That is all 'what-if'. Right now my job is to educate the child. If I am unable to educate the child, then you had better give him to someone who can. You are doing the child an immense disservice by keeping him in my class.

"Some kids may be in special education classes for all their schooling – that's a fact. But there are children who just need a smaller group and they'll only be there for one or two years to get caught up. And it is possible to get caught up. Every child can learn. Ideally I'd put a child with special needs with a teacher who is going to sit with him and tell him what went wrong. He'll be able to get up and walk around – see the fish; do this; do that. He isn't able to just walk around when there are 36 kids in the class. Sounds like the special education, small group environment, is the answer to most of the problems. The kids have access to more resources. The teacher is more approachable. This may not be the complete answer but it is better than we have now."

*Maria:* "I agree. I was taught to pay attention to the individual child. Then I went to work for the school board. You forget all the wonderful ideas. The curriculum becomes the end-all and the be-all. To survive in reality, it is virtually impossible to plan the program to the individual needs of each child. If the child doesn't master the basic skills it is your fault as the teacher, not a problem with the program.

"I think part of the answer is for teachers and consultants to take refresher courses. PD days are not working. I believe IBM, for example, requires their staff to spend one-third of their time in retraining."

*Rosa:* "Workshops aren't necessarily the answer either. People giving workshops think their ideas are the only ones worth anything. They won't listen to any ideas from the floor – or they don't know how. They are usually not geared to helping the teacher. Workshops are usually forums for presenting one individual's ideas."

*Maria:* "Teachers really should be honest with parents about the progress of their child. Parents usually already know, because of what goes on at home, whether or not their child is likely to have problems at school. The teacher will begin to form some impressions about what is going wrong, in grade 1, by Christmas. Certainly by April, the teacher should have very good ideas about the child's individual needs. The teacher should assume responsibility for telling the parents exactly what kind of resources are available for dealing with the problem. Teachers, consultants, parents and informed educational researchers should work together so that children can be helped to experience success."


## Responding to Individual Needs

For several years Benjamin Bloom (1984) and his colleagues have focused their research efforts on many of the concerns expressed by Rosa and Maria. In a word, Bloom wants to bring the benefits of one-to-one tutorials or small group teaching (for two or three students) into large group instruction with about 30 students per teacher. Bloom and his colleagues have shown that with "Mastery Learning" using corrective feedback procedures, where students learn the subject matter in classes with about 30 students per teacher, the average student was about one standard deviation above the average of conventional classes. This means that average mastery learning students were above 84% of the students in conventional classes. With tutoring, the average student was about two standard deviations above the average in conventional classes. This finding is extremely important for learning potential. It shows that most students do have the potential to reach a high level of learning. The primary task set by Bloom and his colleagues is to discover the teaching-learning conditions that will enable the majority of students under group instruction to attain levels of achievement that can at present only be reached under good tutoring conditions.

To summarize from Bloom (1984, p. 5):

> If the research ... yields *practical methods* (methods that the average teacher or school faculty can learn in a brief period of time and use with little more cost or time than conventional instruction), it could be an educational contribution of the greatest magnitude. It would change popular notions about human potential and would have significant effects on what the schools can and should do with the educational years each society requires of its young people.

From our point of view, one of the important contributions in this work is found in the basic assumptions underlying the ML corrective-feedback approach. First, as mentioned above, is the assumption that all students have the potential to attain higher levels of knowledge and understanding than is typically the case in the conventional classroom. Second, is the assumption that there are both cognitive *and* affective prerequisites for each new learning task. Under the ML process, more of the sudents have the cognitive prerequisites for each new task, they become more positive about their ability to learn the subject, and they put in more active learning time than do students in conventional classes. It is not difficult to understand why this is so when one considers some aspects of the ML process. For example, the teacher reteaches items that the majority of students miss, small groups of students help each other over items that have been missed, and students review items they are not sure about by referring to particular pages in the instructional material. Clearly, individual needs are being met in this kind of corrective-feedback process that do not always require the teacher's presence. The primary task of the teacher is to find out what has gone wrong using methods other than giving traditional tests to the students. The attitude here is not one of pass-fail. Rather, the emphasis is on process, as in the question: "How far did you get?"

Bloom and his colleagues have discovered that there is more to learning than the single variable of group instruction. Bloom (1984, p. 15) concludes:

> Early in the work, it became evident that more than group instruction in the school had to be considered. We also needed to find ways of improving the student's learning processes, the curriculum and instructional materials, as well as the home environment support of the students' school learning.

This is indeed a formidable task. In this book we have approached the problem by attempting to describe at least some aspects of intellectual development that have relevance for the learning process. We have also pointed to some emotional correlates of this kind of development. We see them as being interactive. For example the independently secure student will take risks in learning and be responsive to the corrective-feedback approach. Dependently secure students might interpret this kind of feedback as a negative commentary on their learning process since they require approval from others. The independently secure student will usually interpret these comments in the context of constructive criticism.

In this book we emphasize the importance of similarity thinking because we think it constitutes a fundamental prerequisite for significant learning. We believe that the exercise of these thinking skills will enhance the student's initial cognitive entry prerequisites for successful completion of any learning task. In other words, we believe that similarity thinking constitutes general reasoning skills that have application in any learning task. Similarity thinking exercises the higher mental processes which enable students to relate their learning to the many problems they encounter in day-to-day living. Significantly, this way of thinking makes it possible for students to learn how to learn, an essential characteristic needed to cope with a rapidly changing world.

We hope that teachers like Rosa and Maria will be able to use the assessment of similarity thinking in at least two ways. First, to identify and group students on the basis of their performance on similarity thinking and second, to communicate with parents about the significance of their findings. For example, they will be able to describe how this approach is geared to the individual needs of the student, using as guiding criteria how far the student has progressed in similarity thinking. This is important because they will be able to discuss with parents what it means to be able to generalize from the old to the new. We would also expect these teachers to comment on the emotional status of the student, specifically with respect to how the student approaches the learning task. Is the student independently secure? What kinds of activities (both at home and at school) might foster this kind of emotional development? Most important of all we would expect Maria and Rosa to communicate the gist of what we mean by potential to learn, especially the notion of personal best. These are not easy things to do since they are not taught in teacher training courses. But this is no reason for not at least making an attempt in this direction. The next section describes how attitudes about learning can be changed in schools and more generally in various school boards.

## Networking at School and in the Community

You will recall from the Ontario Ministry report at the beginning of the chapter, that in addition to the frustration of responding to individual needs, one of the most troublesome problems experienced by primary teachers is the transition in program and school expectancies for work habits that accompany children as they move from junior kindergarten and kindergarten into grades 1 and 2. Both Maria and Rosa seem to agree with the conclusions of that report, discussing various solutions proposed by school system staff for responding to children whose developmental levels do not correspond to school expectancies which are based on chronological age. This is really the center of the problem. If we are not alerted early on to the child's developing thinking or learning skills it is impossible to provide appropriate transition experiences. Furthermore, we are led to the question, transition to what? Surely, if our objective is to help children realize their potential to learn and in so doing, learn how to learn, opportunities for learning should not differ in kind across the entire spectrum of school experience from junior kindergarten on.

We take the view in this book that our goal as educators is very clear and specific. It is to take account of the child's potential to learn as early as possible, including both cognitive skills and emotional maturity, the latter understood particularly with respect to the development of independent security. On this view some children are ready (in terms of their learning skills and emotional maturity), to learn how to read and/or begin to understand number concepts as early as junior kindergarten. Other children may not be "ready" for these activities until grade 2 or later.

120

It is not impossible to accommodate these kinds of individual differences and needs in contemporary school settings. In this book we have suggested a means toward achieving groupings of students based on both cognitive and emotional developmental criteria. Current attempts at early identification are simply too piecemeal to convey an accurate picture of the child's potential to learn. In our view the model of similarity thinking, as well as our notions about what constitutes emotional maturity, make this kind of comprehensive picture a possibility. Obviously, considerable work remains to be done by school system staff to implement this approach. With this end in view we have enlisted the support of one school board in Ontario which is ready to make this proposal a reality in a demonstration setting in one school from junior kindergarten through grade 2.

How does the teacher makes a contribution in this proposal? Maria and Rosa have both talked about not getting respect from other school staff. For example they are understandably concerned that their observations always seem to need to be checked out and verified by other, presumably more qualified personnel. This situation obviously begs the question about the teacher's domain of expertise and about teacher training in general.

In our view teachers need to take a position about the learning process and the kinds of objectives that can be realized when the learning process is stimulated. This book at the very least will help teachers consolidate their views on this issue. The practical consequences of this are enormous. For example consider the consequence of adopting the view that learning potential should take into account the student's perceptions of his or her personal best. This view will require a reconsideration of learning that is "lock-step", tied as it is to examination results. This view also requires a reconsideration of learning outcomes as well as curriculum objectives that are set as a function of the student's chronological age. Instead, the teacher begins to set learning objectives according to the student's current learning skills and level of emotional maturity. The important idea here is that teachers really must be able to express a point of view about learning and we would hope about what it means to have the potential to learn. Rosa has a very good point when she suggests that workshops are not always that productive. However, once teachers have a definite agenda about what it is that they want to learn, workshops can take on a new significance. For example rather than simply listening to various theories about cognitive and emotional development teachers can insist that these theories be related to specific problems, like how to group students in such a way that both learning and emotional skills are taken into account. Essentially, they will have put on their agenda how to meet the individual needs of their students.

In a word, teachers can take responsibility for initiating contact with resource personnel, whether that resource is available in the school board itself or elsewhere. If teachers want to have respect it would seem that they will have to proceed with something like this kind of agenda.

This sort of initiative is at the roots of the networking concept. The professional teacher is in our view responsible for focusing the resources of the school system and community on individual student needs. Having a point of view about learning means that the teacher will be able to coordinate the resources offered by several kinds of consultants around individual needs. In this role the teacher is able to reach out to the home and the community. The professional teacher is on this view one who understands what the family, community and consultant specialist has to offer to make a significant difference to each student's learning process.

This is not an impossible task. We have taken a first step in this book by providing you with a point of view about learning. We hope that it has made a difference to your learning process. We wait upon your comments to respond to your individual needs.

122

# REFERENCES

Allan, G.D. *Counting and part-whole relational information in children's judgements of numerosity.* Unpublished doctoral dissertation, University of Toronto, 1984.

Arthur, G. A non-verbal test of logical thinking. *Journal of Consulting Psychology,* 1944, *8,* 33-34.

Blatz, W. *Understanding the young child.* Toronto: Clarke Irwin & Co, 1944.

Bloom, B.S. The 2 sigma problem: The search for methods of group instruction as effective as one-to-one tutoring. *Educational Researcher,* 1984, *13,* No. 6.

Davis, C. *Room to grow.* Toronto: University of Toronto Press, 1966.

Douglas, V.I. Stop look and listen: A problem of sustained attention and impulse control in hyperactive and normal children. *Canadian Journal of Behaviour Science,* 1972, *4,* 259-281.

Douglas, V.I. Differences between normal and hyperkinetic children. In C. J. Conners (Ed.), *Clinical use of stimulant drugs in children.* Princeton, New Jersey: Excerptamedica, 1974.

Djap, D.P. *Proverbial understanding and the development of part-whole reasoning skills.* Unpublished doctoral dissertation,University of Toronto, 1983.

Egeland, B. Training impulsive children in the use of more efficient scanning techniques. *Child Development,* 1974, *45,* 165-171.

Erikson, E.H. Identity and the life cycle. *Psychological Issues,* 1959, *1,* 18-164.

Erikson, E.H. *Childhood and society* (rev. ed.). New York: Norton, 1963.

Fleming, D.R. *The effects of audience on the expressive language of working-class children.* Unpublished doctoral dissertation, University of Toronto, 1979.

Gamlin, P.J. *The development of number concepts.* Paper presented at the 1982 Biennial University of Waterloo Conference on Child Development, Waterloo, Ontario, Canada, 1982.

Gamlin, P.J., & Tramposch, F.R. *Proverbial understanding and the development of metaphorical thinking.* Paper presented at the Convention of the Canadian Psychological Association, Toronto, 1981.

Johnson, D.J. Process deficits in learning disabled children and implications for reading. In L. B. Resnick & P. A. Weaver (Eds.), *Theory and practice of early reading* (Vol. 1). Hillsdale, NJ: Erlbaum, 1979.

Kinsbourne, M., & Caplan, P. *Children's learning and attention problems.* Boston: Little, Brown & Co., 1979.

Kogan, N., Connor, K., Gross, A., & Fava, D. Understanding visual metaphor: Developmental and individual differences. *Monographs of the Society for Research in Child Development,* 1980, *45* (1, Serial No. 183).

Orme, M. *Strategies of effective teaching.* Toronto: Ontario Educational Communications Authority, 1978.

Rizwan, S. *Part-whole information and children's number concepts.* Unpublished doctoral dissertation, University of Toronto, 1984.

Robertson, M.L. *Teaching strategies to enhance children's reflective reasoning processes.* Unpublished doctoral dissertation, University of Toronto, 1985.

Ross, A. *Psychological aspects of learning disabilities and reading disorders.* Toronto: McGraw-Hill, 1976.

Vulpé, S.G. *Vulpé Assessment Battery.* National Institute of Mental Retardation, 1979.

Vygotsky, L.S. *Thought and language.* Cambridge, MA: M.I.T. Press, 1962.

# APPENDIX

## Scripts for Microteaching Videotapes

Have you ever been in a situation like this?

Mother is sick. All of the kids agree to pitch in and help. Jane starts a wash with white clothes in hot water. Jack, thinking that he is being helpful, throws in all of his dirty clothes including his dark red hockey shirt. The colour from Jack's shirt runs and the whole wash comes out pink including previously white clothes. Now Jack has pink underwear.

This story might be an instance of "Too many cooks spoil the soup."

Or, how about this situation?

You have just caught a toad. You want to keep him close to you so you turn a large jar filled with grass, stones and insects into his home. However you forget to punch holes in the lid of the jar. Mother discovers the dead toad when she goes in search of the rotten smell in your bedroom. You are very upset because your mistake has meant the loss of your pet. Mother comforts you and says, "Don't cry over spilt milk."

Does anyone know what we call "Too many cooks spoil the soup" and "Don't cry over spilt milk"?

The term we are going to use to describe these sayings is the term *proverb*. A proverb is a short sentence not a whole story. Proverbs offer advice or a word of wisdom or teach a lesson. They are similar to fairy tales because there is usually a moral to go along with them.

What have we said about proverbs so far?

Can you give me an example of a proverb? Try to recall the proverbs mentioned before.

Example 1

How about a different example?

Example 2

Let's focus on the proverb, "It's no good crying over spilt milk."

125

# Script for Microteaching Videotape: Reflective Reasoning Condition

Would you only hear the proverb "It's no good crying over spilt milk" in a situation where milk has been spilt?

(If a prompt is necessary refer to the dead toad example.)

In what other situations might you hear someone use this proverb?

Given what you have said so far, is spilling milk the same as making a mistake?

Good, you have already given me examples of other mistakes which might lead someone to use the proverb. You've mentioned

(example 1 and example 2)

Let us take this one step further – What does the proverb tell us to do when we make mistakes?

Here is a summary of a couple of meanings to go with the proverb "It's no good crying over spilt milk":

1. After you have spilt milk do something better than crying about it.

2. After you have made a mistake do something better than worrying about it.

Did you notice any differences in the wording in the two meanings for the proverbs?

What do the two meanings have in common?

(If prompt is necessary, "Do both meanings go with the proverb?")

In summary, then, the paraphrase meaning "After you have made a mistake do something better than worrying about it" says the same thing as the proverb "It's no good crying over spilt milk" without using the same words. It is also a more general way of saying what the proverb means and it refers to more situations than just spilling milk.

Let us put together everything that we have done so far by working through this exercise:

*It's no good crying over spilt milk*

1. After you have spilt milk do something better than crying about it.

126

2. After you have made a mistake worrying about it may help.

3. After you have made a mistake do something better than worrying about it.

4. After you have spilt milk crying about it is a good thing to do.

Which two paraphrases mean the same as the proverb?

Which of these two paraphrases tells you the moral of the proverb?

Therefore, which one of the two paraphrases (meanings) is the best one?

## Script for Microteaching Videotape: Detail Oriented Condition

Let us try to figure out what the proverb is trying to tell us.

Does the proverb say that crying is a good thing to do after spilling milk?

What does the proverb recommend that you do after spilling milk?

Is there another way of saying the same thing as "It's no good crying over spilt milk"?

Would you say that "After you have spilt milk do something better than crying about it" means the same as the proverb?

How do you know that "After you have spilt milk do something better than crying about it" is a correct paraphrase of the proverb?

In summary, then, the paraphrase "After you have spilt milk do something better than crying about it" means the same as the proverb "It's no good crying over spilt milk" and uses many of the same words as the proverb but not all of them.

Would the paraphrase "After you have made a mistake do something better than worrying about it" mean the same as proverb too?

Let us put together everything that we have done so far by working through this exercise:

*It's no good crying over spilt milk*

1. After you have spilt milk do something better than crying about it.

2. After you have made a mistake worrying about it may help.

3. After you have made a mistake do something better than worrying about it.

4. After you have spilt milk crying about it is a good thing to do.

During the in-class, teacher question/student response interactions that followed the videotape, the questions were virtually identical to those on the Reflective Reasoning Condition Tape or the Detail Oriented Condition Tape except that they were based on another common proverb "Too many cooks spoil the soup."

# Author Index

# Subject Index